DK EYEWITNESS

T0043290

TOP **10**
LISBON

Top 10 Lisbon Highlights

The Top 10 of Everything

CONTENTS

Lisbon Area by Area

Streetsmart

Within each Top 10 list in this book, no hierarchy of quality or popularity is implied. All 10 are, in the editor's opinion, of roughly equal merit.
Title page, front cover and spine *The historic neighbourhood of Alfama, Lisbon*
Back cover, clockwise from top left *Queluz National Palace; Sé de Lisboa; Baixa district; Praça do Comercio; skyline*

The rapid rate at which the world is changing is constantly keeping the DK Eyewitness team on our toes. While we've worked hard to ensure that this edition of Lisbon is accurate and up-to-date, we know that opening hours alter, standards shift, prices fluctuate, places close and new ones pop up in their stead. So, if you notice we've got something wrong or left something out, we want to hear about it. Please get in touch at **travelguides@dk.com**

Welcome to
Lisbon

Lisbon is a city of superlatives: the most westerly capital in mainland Europe, one of the sunniest, one of the least expensive and – draped over a series of hills facing the Tejo estuary – surely one of the most impressively located. With DK Eyewitness Top 10 Lisbon, it's yours to explore.

Lisbon's position just inland from the Atlantic helped it become the centre of a historic maritime empire that stretched from Brazil to Indonesia. The legacy is a flamboyant architecture typified by the Manueline structures of the riverside **Torre de Belém** and the magnificent **Mosteiro dos Jerónimos**. There's also an older, Moorish aspect to the warren of streets of the **Alfama** district, below the stunning hilltop **Castelo de São Jorge** and the medieval **Sé**. Lisbon's museums are equally diverse, from the historic works of art in the **Museu Nacional de Arte Antiga** to the panoply of international masterpieces in the **Museu Calouste Gulbenkian**.

Lisbon oozes history and tradition, but it is anything but staid. Nights out in the **Bairro Alto** or **Cais do Sodré** districts are memorable and there's a vibrancy to the city's street cafés and restaurants that's hard to match. Among the quaint old trams and cobbled streets, you'll also find some eye-catching modern architecture, typified by the futuristic **Parque das Nações**, which contains one of Europe's largest oceanariums.

Whether you're coming for a weekend or a week, our Top 10 guide brings together everything the city has to offer, from the coolest clubs to the best nearby beaches. There are tips throughout, from finding out what's free to uncovering the city's best beaches, plus eight easy-to-follow itineraries, designed to cover a range of sights in a short space of time. Add inspiring photography and detailed maps, and you've got the essential pocket-sized travel companion. **Enjoy the book, and enjoy Lisbon.**

Clockwise from top: *Neptune and Amphitrite in a Chariot*, Museu Nacional do Azulejo; tower at Quinta da Regaleira, Sintra; vaulted ceiling, Mosteiro dos Jerónimos; Torre de São Lourenço, Castelo de São Jorge; view from Castelo de São Jorge; Guincho beach; Portas do Sol viewpoint

Exploring Lisbon

It's great fun travelling around Lisbon, especially by tram or bus, which will take you to most of the city's historical buildings, parks and museums. Whether you're coming for a weekend, or want to get to know the city better, these two- and four-day itineraries will help you to make the most of your visit.

The views from the Castelo de São Jorge are some of Lisbon's finest.

Mosteiro dos Jerónimos features an elaborate façade.

Key
— Two-day itinerary
— Four-day itinerary

Two Days in Lisbon

Day **❶**
MORNING
From the Baixa district, take the famous tram 28 to the **Sé de Lisboa** *(see pp16–17)*. After exploring its ancient interior, continue to the hilltop **Castelo de São Jorge** *(see pp12–13)*, a Moorish castle offering fantastic views over the city.

AFTERNOON
Head north to the **Museu Calouste Gulbenkian** *(see pp30–31)*. Housed in a modern cultural centre in attractive grounds, the museum displays an astonishing array of art – from ancient times to the 20th century.

Museu Nacional de Arte Antiga displays an exquisite collection of Portuguese art.

Day **❷**
MORNING
Head west along the riverfront to the **Museu Nacional de Arte Antiga** *(see pp18–19)*. Set in a former palace, the museum contains paintings, furniture and other works of decorative art.

AFTERNOON
Travel west to the riverside suburb of Belém. Close to the stunning 16th-century **Mosteiro dos Jerónimos** *(see pp14–15)* stands the iconic **Torre de Belém** *(see pp22–3)*, built in the ornate Manueline style.

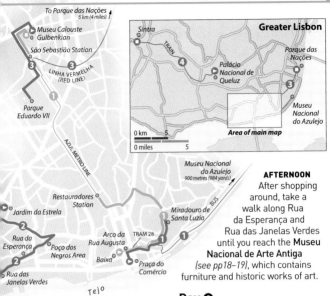

Four Days in Lisbon

Day ❶
MORNING

Take a stroll along Lisbon's riverfront, passing through the grand square of **Praça do Comércio** *(see p69)*. Climb up the nearby **Arco da Rua Augusta** *(see p43)* for a wonderful panoramic view of the city. Then head to the bougainvillea-framed **Miradouro de Santa Luzia** *(see p42)* and get lost in Alfama's maze of streets.

AFTERNOON

Take a bus east to the **Museu Nacional do Azulejo** *(see pp26-7)* to appreciate the amazing diversity of ceramic tiles *(azulejos)* that you'll see on many of the city's buildings. The museum is located inside the exquisite Madre de Deus convent.

Day ❷
MORNING

Spend the morning exploring the **Jardim da Estrela** *(see p57)*, stopping to visit the nearby basilica *(see p40)*. Then head down to the creative **Poço dos Negros Area** *(see p47)* for a coffee and a few cool souvenirs.

AFTERNOON

After shopping around, take a walk along Rua da Esperança and Rua das Janelas Verdes until you reach the **Museu Nacional de Arte Antiga** *(see pp18-19)*, which contains furniture and historic works of art.

Day ❸
MORNING

Take the metro to **Museu Calouste Gulbenkian** *(see pp30-31)*, which houses an internationally acclaimed collection of artworks spanning 4,000 years of art history. Then head to the sloping Parque Eduardo VII for fine views over the city.

AFTERNOON

Travel northeast on the metro to the **Parque das Nações** *(see pp20-21)*, a district built for Lisbon's Expo 98. It offers a cable car, a science museum, riverside walks and one of Europe's largest oceanariums.

Day ❹
MORNING

Take a train from the city to the **Palácio Nacional de Queluz** *(see pp28-9)*, where the gardens and interiors show the lavish lifestyle enjoyed by the Portuguese royals.

AFTERNOON

Continue on the train to the village of Sintra *(see pp32-3)*, a favoured summer hideaway for artists, monarchs and the wealthy. Much of it designated a UNESCO World Heritage Site, its highlights include the Palácio Nacional da Pena and Castelo dos Mouros.

Top 10 Lisbon Highlights

Interior at Palácio Nacional de Queluz

🔟 Lisbon Highlights

One of the oldest cities in Europe, Lisbon is steeped in history. The city's rich past can be uncovered in its imposing palaces and impressive churches, as well as in its enticing art- and artifact-filled museums. But Lisbon also has a playful side, thanks to its contemporary art galleries and vibrant nightlife scene.

① Castelo de São Jorge
Crowning the hill where Lisbon's original settlers lived, this evocatively restored medieval castle affords fabulous views *(see pp12–13)*.

Mosteiro dos Jerónimos ②
The Manueline is Portugal's own architectural style. Some of its greatest expressions can be seen in this glorious monastery *(see pp14–15)*.

BAIRRO DA AJUDA · Jardim Botânico da Ajuda
ALTO DA AJUDA
RESTELO
Jardim Botânico Tropical
SANTO AMARO
AVE DA TORRE DE BELÉM
BELÉM ②
AVENIDA DA ÍNDIA
AVENIDA DA ÍNDIA
PONTE 25 DE ABRIL

0 km — 1
0 miles — 1

③ Sé de Lisboa
Lisbon's cathedral was built in the middle of the 12th century, just after the Christian reconquest. It is a fortress-like structure with stonework that glows amber as the sun sets *(see pp16–17)*.

④ Museu Nacional de Arte Antiga
Housed in a grand 17th-century palace, Portugal's national gallery displays a treasure trove of art, and places the country in historical context through its exhibits *(see pp18–19)*.

⑤ Parque das Nações
Flanked by the Vasco da Gama Bridge, the site of Lisbon's sea-themed Expo 98 has been transformed into a dynamic leisure, business and residential area *(see pp20–21)*.

⑥ Torre de Belém

The defensive tower at Belém is one of Lisbon's emblems, and one of the most perfectly proportioned examples of the Manueline style *(see pp22–3)*.

⑦ Museu Nacional do Azulejo

This museum is devoted to the quintessential Portuguese decorative element – the tile. It is also set in a stunning convent *(see pp26–7)*.

Greater Lisbon

⑧ Palácio Nacional de Queluz

A Rococo feast, this summer palace just outside Lisbon was briefly the royal family's permanent residence. It exudes an air of ordered pleasure *(see pp28–9)*.

Museu Calouste Gulbenkian ⑨

A museum of international calibre, the Gulbenkian is a small and pleasant universe of art history *(see pp30–31)*.

Sintra ⑩

Sintra draws countless visitors with its picturesque palaces and castle. Lord Byron and the Portuguese royalty made these mountains their summer retreat *(see pp32–3)*.

TOP 10 ⭐ Castelo de São Jorge

This hilltop castle is traditionally regarded as the site of Lisbon's founding settlement. Archaeological finds dated to the 7th century BC support this theory, although the oldest castle remains are from the Moorish era. Portugal's first king, Afonso Henriques, captured the Moorish citadel in 1147 and his successors added the Alcáçovas palace, which remained the royal residence until 1511. Following centuries of neglect, the castle was imaginatively restored in 1938, providing the city with one of its most attractive viewpoints.

The restored battlements at Castelo de São Jorge

1 Porta de São Jorge

This grand gate leads onto the final steep climb up to the castle grounds. In a wall niche to the left is a figure of St George. His local connection may derive from the role played by English troops in the conquest of Moorish Lisbon.

2 Torre da Igreja

On Largo de Santa Cruz do Castelo is this 18th-century church tower. The building was closed and largely forgotten until 2018, when it opened to visitors. A separate ticket gives you access to the top, from where you can enjoy incredible city views.

3 Castle Museum

On the site of the Alcáçovas palace, the museum **(left)** contains a collection of artifacts excavated from the hilltop, such as Iron Age cooking pots and 15th-century tiles.

4 Torre de Ulisses

In one of the inner battlement towers, a camera obscura attached to a periscope projects images of the city. The castle has a history of distant gazing: Lisbon's first observatory was set up there in c 1788.

5 Torre de São Lourenço

Connected to the castle by a long series of steps **(left)**, this tower once formed part of the outer fortifications. Today, it offers another angle from which to view the castle.

6 Santa Cruz Neighbourhood

The tiny neighbourhood of Santa Cruz do Castelo, within the old citadel, is one of the most picturesque parts of Lisbon. It is home to cafés, guesthouses and a viewpoint overlooking Alfama.

PORTA DE MARTIM MONIZ

According to legend, the knight Martim Moniz prevented this gate from closing with his own body, sacrificing his life to allow Afonso Henriques and his troops to storm the castle. The gate where his unverified deed took place bears his name, as does a square below the castle.

7 Inner Battlements

The reconstruction of the inner castle is one of the great achievements of the 1938 restoration. With ten towers and a dividing inner wall, the restored castle closely matches the layout and size of the original.

8 Archaeological Site

This site features traces of the most significant periods in Lisbon's history, including settlements from the Iron Age.

10 Esplanade

The esplanade **(above)** on top of the outer fortifications is one of the main rewards of a climb up to the castle. Dotted with archaeological remains and shaded by pines, it follows the castle's western perimeter, offering views of the river and lower city.

Map of Castelo de São Jorge

50 metres (55 yards)

FLORES DE S. CRUZ
S. CRUZ DO CASTELO
RECOLHIMENTO

⑤ ④ ③ ⑩ ⑨ ① ⑧ ⑦ ② ⑥

NEED TO KNOW

MAP G4 ■ Porta de São Jorge, Rua de Santa Cruz do Castelo ■ 218 800 620 ■ www.castelodesaojorge.pt

Main castle complex: 9am–9pm daily (Nov–Feb: to 6pm)

Torre de Ulisses camera obscura: 10am–5pm daily

Torre da Igreja: 10am–1pm & 2–7pm daily; adm: €2.5; www.torreda igrejadocastelo.pt

Castle museum: 9am–9pm daily (Nov–Feb: to 6pm); adm: €10; concessions €5–€8.50; under-12s free

■ The west-facing esplanade is best in the late afternoon.

■ The outdoor bar at Chapitô *(see p66)* is a good place to relax.

9 Statue of Afonso Henriques

This bronze statue of Portugal's first king **(right)** was added to the esplanade in 1947. It is a copy of an 1887 work by Soares dos Reis (the original is in Guimarães).

TOP 10 ⭐ Mosteiro dos Jerónimos

Few of Lisbon's monuments are overly grand, and while this historic monastery is imposing, it's easy to explore. Begun in the early 16th century by Diogo de Boytac and finished by João de Castilho and Jerónimo de Ruão, Jerónimos signifies Portugal's territorial expansion and expresses a uniquely national style. Construction of the building was funded by a spice tax imposed after Vasco da Gama landed in India. The monastery has a cenotaph honouring him and other notable Portuguese nationals, including the poet Luís de Camões.

1 South Portal
Restraint might not be the word for this towering sculpture of an entrance **(left)**, but look closely and you'll see that none of its parts is overpoweringly large. The figures include Henry the Navigator.

2 Nave
Many visitors find the well-lit nave **(right)** the most striking feature of Jerónimos, with its soaring carved pillars supporting a beautiful fan-vaulted ceiling.

NEED TO KNOW

MAP B6 ■ Praça do Império, Belém ■ 213 620 034 ■ www.mosteiro jeronimos.gov.pt

Open 10am–6:30pm Tue–Sun (Oct–Apr: to 5:30pm). Closed 1 Jan, Easter Sun, 1 May, 13 Jun, 24–25 Dec

Adm: €10; concessions €5; under-12s free

■ This is one of the most visited sites in Lisbon. Think twice before going at weekends, or mid-mornings or mid-afternoons (the latter two are favoured by tour groups). Hit it at lunchtime, or just before it closes, when the stone turns honey-coloured.

■ After your visit, grab a bite to eat at nearby Pão Pão Queijo Queijo *(see p89)*, and dine on the terrace overlooking the monastery.

3 West Portal
The surrounds of this portal (now the main entrance) were sculpted by Nicolau Chanterène, and show the Manueline love of fantastical Renaissance decoration.

4 Cloister
The unique two-storey cloister is a lesson in Manueline tracery and lavish ornament **(above)**. Fernando Pessoa *(see p85)*, the renowned poet, is buried in the cloister.

5 Refectory

The long, narrow refectory features fabulous vaulting and rope-like Manueline mouldings. The panel on the north wall **(left)** depicts the biblical story of the feeding of the 5,000.

STONE SURPRISES

Spend some time studying the carvings on the pillars in the nave and you will come across plants and animals, along with exquisite human faces, and a few mythical figures. What better way to remind posterity that all this beauty was hewn by human hands, belonging to individuals who might occasionally let their imaginations roam free while carving.

6 Tombs of Dom Sebastião and Cardinal D. Henrique

As you pass under the stellar vault of the crossing, look to each side to see the grand tombs of Cardinal D. Henrique and the young king Dom Sebastião.

7 Chapterhouse

Completed only in the 19th century, the attractive chapterhouse was never used as such. It houses the tomb of Alexandre Herculano, a celebrated 19th-century historian who also served as the first mayor of Belém.

8 Main Chapel

The current main chapel, dating from 1572, has a grid-like Mannerist layout. Look out for the tombs of Dom Manuel I and his wife Dona Maria (on the left) and Dom João III and his wife Dona Catarina (on the right).

9 Extension

Major restoration works in the 19th century added the long, Neo-Manueline west wing, which now houses the Museu de Arqueologia (closed for renovation until 2025) and part of the Museu de Marinha. A distinctive domed bell tower was built to replace the previous pointed roof.

Plan of Mosteiro dos Jerónimos

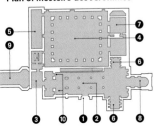

10 Tombs of Vasco da Gama and Luís de Camões

In the Lower Choir – facing the aisles under the gallery – are the tombs of Vasco da Gama **(above)** and Luís de Camões, transferred here in 1898.

🔟 ⭐ Sé de Lisboa

Lisbon's cathedral was built shortly after Afonso Henriques had taken Lisbon from the Moors in 1147, and stands on a site once occupied by the city's main mosque. Today's crenellated Romanesque building is a much-restored reconstruction, rebuilt in various architectural styles following earthquake damage. It is also an archaeological site, with new finds made regularly beneath the cloister – originally excavated to reinforce the building's foundations.

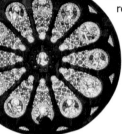

4 Treasury
The first-floor Treasury is a museum of religious art, with some important holdings. It lost its greatest treasure, the relics of St Vincent *(see p40)*, in the 1755 earthquake.

6 Cloister
The Gothic cloister, reached through one of the chapels, was an early addition to the cathedral. Some of its decoration anticipates the Manueline style. It is currently closed for restoration.

1 Rose Window
Reconstructed using parts of the original, the rose window **(above)** softens the façade's rather severe aspect. It depicts Jesus surrounded by the 12 apostles.

2 Bell Towers
These stocky towers – defining features of the Sé de Lisboa – recall those of Coimbra's earlier cathedral, built by the same master builder, Frei Roberto. A taller third tower collapsed during the 1755 earthquake *(see p36)*.

3 St Anthony's Font

Tradition has it that Fernando Martins Bulhões (later St Anthony) was baptized in this font, which now features a tile panel of the saint preaching to the fishes. He is also said to have attended the cathedral school.

5 Gothic Ambulatory Chapels
The Chapel of São Cosme and São Damião is one of nine along the ambulatory. Look out for the tombs of nobleman Lopo Fernandes Pacheco **(below)** and his wife, Maria Villalobos.

7 Romanesque Nave

Little remains of the original cathedral beyond the renovated nave **(above)**. It leads to a chancel enclosed by an ambulatory, a 14th-century addition.

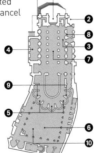

Plan of Sé de Lisboa

The bell towers of the Sé de Lisboa

FINDS FROM LISBON'S PAST

Archaeologically, the Sé de Lisboa is a work in progress – just like the castle *(see pp12–13)* and many other parts of central Lisbon. All this digging means that an increasing number of ancient remains are being uncovered. Public information can lag behind archaeological breakthroughs, but make a point of asking – you may be treated to a glimpse of the latest discovery.

9 13th-century Iron Railing

One of the ambulatory chapels is closed off by a 13th-century iron railing, the only one of its kind to survive in Portugal.

8 Capela de Bartolomeu Joanes

This Gothic chapel, sponsored by a Lisbon merchant in 1324, has the founder's tomb and a 15th-century Renaissance retable, painted by Cristóvão de Figueiredo, Garcia Fernandes and Diogo de Contreiras.

10 Archaeological Finds

Remains left by Moors, Visigoths, Romans and Phoenicians have been found in the excavation of the cloister **(above)**.

NEED TO KNOW

MAP G4 ■ Largo da Sé
■ 218 866 752

Church: 9:30am–7pm Mon–Sat (Oct–May: 10am–6pm Mon–Sat)

Adm: €5; concessions €3

■ The Sé de Lisboa is a very dark church, and much of interest in the chapels is literally obscured. Head for the lighter cloister, and try to go in the afternoon, when the low light enters the façade's rose window.

■ A great place for a relaxed drink in the neighbourhood is the charming Crafty Corner *(see p66)*, which serves Lisbon craft beer in a medieval-style setting.

TOP 10 ⭐ Museu Nacional de Arte Antiga

Lisbon's Museu Nacional de Arte Antiga (MNAA) is Portugal's national gallery, a treasure trove of historically illuminating art. Housed in a 17th-century palace overlooking the river and port area, the museum was inaugurated in 1884. Today it contains a vast selection of European art dating from the 14th to the 19th centuries, and includes the most complete collection of Portuguese works in the world.

1 The Panels of St Vincent

A key Portuguese painting, this polyptych of around 1470 (probably by Nuno Gonçalves) portrays rich and poor in fascinating detail.

2 Martyrdom of St Sebastian

Painted by Gregório Lopes around 1536, this work was a part of a group of paintings intended to be placed on the altars of the Rotunda of the Convento de Cristo.

4 Portuguese and Chinese Ceramics

The museum's 7,500-piece collection of ceramics illustrates the interplay of international trade influences. From the 16th century, Portuguese faïence displays traces of Ming, while Chinese porcelain includes Portuguese coats of arms and other similar motifs.

5 Indo-Portuguese Furniture

The most interesting of the museum's furniture collections is probably the group of Indo-Portuguese pieces. The *contadores* **(left)** are many-drawered chests that combine orderliness with decorative abandon.

3 Chapel of St Albert

Decorated with *azulejos* and gilded wood carving, this chapel is a prime example of Portuguese Baroque.

NEED TO KNOW

MAP E5 ▪ Rua das Janelas Verdes ▪ 213 912 800 ▪ www.museudearteantiga.pt

Open 10am–6pm Tue–Sun; closed 1 Jan, Easter Sun, 1 May, 13 Jun, 25 Dec

Adm: €6; concessions €3; under-12s free

▪ Until 2023, the Panels of St Vincent will be undergoing restoration. Despite this the panels will still be on show, with visitors able to watch the live restoration taking place via a viewing window on the museum's third floor.

▪ An alternative to the museum restaurant for lunch or dinner is the rooftop bar Le Chat, which offers breathtaking views, live music and good cocktails (Jardim 9 de Abril).

6 Namban Screens

After encountering Portuguese travellers in the 16th century, Japan's artists portrayed them as *namban-jin*, or "southern barbarians". These screens **(below)** depict the arrival of Portuguese ships in the port of Nagasaki.

8 St Jerome

This unusual portrait transcends the conventions of religious art. Painted in 1521 by Albrecht Dürer – who used a 93-year-old man from Antwerp as his model – it is above all a powerful portrayal of wisdom and old age.

LA NUIT DES MUSÉES

If you are in Lisbon in May, visit this museum at night to enjoy a programme of concerts and other events – not least the guided evening tours. Part of a Europe-wide French initiative to make museum visits more than occasional Sunday afternoon outings, Noite dos Museus gives access to the museum's treasures in a quite different context.

9 The Temptations of St Anthony

Hieronymus Bosch's three-panelled feast of fear and fantasy **(below)**, painted around 1500, is one of the museum's great treasures – and one of the world's great paintings.

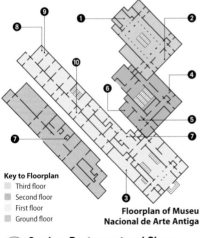

Key to Floorplan
- Third floor
- Second floor
- First floor
- Ground floor

Floorplan of Museu Nacional de Arte Antiga

7 Garden, Restaurant and Shop

The museum's restaurant has lovely views of the garden and the river. There is a well-stocked gift shop on the first floor.

10 Conversation

Pieter de Hooch was a genre painter whose treatment of light was perhaps more complex than that of his contemporary, Vermeer. This work shows his key qualities as an artist.

TOP 10 ★ Parque das Nações

Built on the site of Lisbon's Expo 98 world exposition, held to mark the 500th anniversary of Vasco da Gama's voyage to India, the "Park of Nations" is a modern, self-contained riverside district east of the centre. It showcases contemporary Portuguese architecture, in stark contrast to the Manueline extravaganzas of historic Lisbon and Belém. A bustling amusement park and trade-fair centre by day, by night the park becomes a lively concert and events venue.

1 Cable Car
Running most of the length of the Parque, the cable car (above) gives an overview of the area and views of the river and Vasco da Gama bridge. If the breeze is up, the cars may swing from side to side.

2 Torre Vasco da Gama
At 145 m (476 ft), this is Lisbon's tallest building, albeit removed from the rest of the urban skyline. It is now part of a hotel with a Michelin-star restaurant on the top floor.

3 Nautical Centre
The Doca dos Olivais nautical centre rents out equipment for various water sports and related activities.

4 Oceanário de Lisboa
This is one of Europe's largest aquariums (above). It has hundreds of aquatic species which are organized by habitat and viewed on two levels. The central tank has species large and small, but it's the sea otters in a side tank that get the most attention.

5 Restaurants
There are over 40 waterfront restaurants, many with outdoor seating. Popular for weekend lunches, they also form part of the Parque's nightlife scene.

6 Casino
A newer addition to the Parque, in the former Future Pavilion, the casino caters to all gamblers, offering slot machines, poker, roulette and blackjack.

7 Shops

Most shops **(left)** are in the Vasco da Gama centre, but there are also electronics and home interiors showrooms elsewhere in the Parque. People come to see the latest offers when the FIL trade-fair area puts on a consumer show.

CARD ADVANTAGES

The Lisboa Card ranges in price from €21 (valid for 24 hours) to €44 (72 hours). It provides free transport on the entire network (including the lifts and the train from Rossio to Sintra) and free entry to 37 places of interest. The card, which covers one adult, can be bought online at www. visitlisboa.com. A separate card is available for kids aged 4 to 15.

Map of Parque das Nações

NEED TO KNOW

MAP D1 ■ Avenida Dom João II

Oceanário de Lisboa: 218 917 000; open 10am–8pm daily (last entry 7pm); adm: €22; senior €17; 3–12 years €15; www.oceanario.pt

Knowledge Pavilion – Ciência Viva: 218 917 100; open 10am–6pm Tue–Fri, 11am–7pm Sat & Sun (book tickets online in advance); adm: €11; under-18s €9; over-65s €8; children 3–11 €8; under-2s free (family ticket available); www.pavconhe cimento.pt

Casino: www.casino-lisboa.pt

■ Summer afternoons are hotter and more humid than in most of the city. The lawn next to Oceanário de Lisboa and the riverfront benches are good spots to rest.

8 Knowledge Pavilion – Ciência Viva

This large, child-friendly science museum is full of interactive multimedia exhibits, simulations, experiments and activities for various age groups, using cutting-edge technology.

9 Portugal Pavilion

With its concrete canopy suspended like a sail above the forecourt, the Portugal Pavilion **(below)** was once going to house the Council of Ministers. The space is currently used for special events and temporary exhibitions.

10 Gardens

Many of the rather anaemic-looking gardens planted for Expo 98 have grown into healthy patches of urban greenery, effectively softening the concrete and steel, particularly along the waterfront.

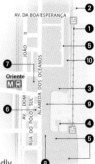

TOP 10 ★ Torre de Belém

The defensive tower at Belém is a jewel of the Manueline architectural style, combining Moorish, Renaissance and Gothic elements in a dazzling whole. It was built in 1514–20 by Francisco de Arruda, probably to a design by Diogo de Boytac. At that time, the tower stood on an island in the river Tejo, about 200 m (650 ft) from the northern bank, commanding the approach to Lisbon. The land between the tower and the Jerónimos monastery has since been reclaimed.

1 Battlements
The merlons of most of the tower's battlements are decorated with the cross of the Order of Christ, carved to look like features on a shield. The smaller merlons at the rear and on top of the tower are crowned with pyramid-shaped spikes.

2 Watchtowers
You can't miss the Moorish-influenced watchtowers **(below)**. Their domes are seated on Manueline rope-like circles and rise to a pile of small spheres reminiscent of the tops of chess pieces.

Dazzling carved exterior of the Torre de Belém

3 Exhibitions
The tower's former dungeon, now quite bright, is often used for temporary exhibitions, as well as for a permanent information display for visitors and a gift shop.

4 Virgin and Child Sculpture
A statue of Our Lady of Safe Homecoming stands by the light well that was used to lower cannons into the dungeon. She evokes memories of both Portugal's era of exploration and of those away at sea – and of the concerned longing for absent husbands and sons known in Portugal as *saudade*.

5 Governor's Room
Now empty, this room was used by the tower's first governor, Gaspar de Paiva. After it became obsolete, lighthouse keepers and customs officials worked here. The room's acoustics amplify even the slightest whisper.

6 Rhinoceros Detail
Each of the sentry boxes is supported by a naturalistically carved stone. The rhinoceros on the northwestern box is the most famous, thought to be the first European carving of this animal. Time has now rounded its features.

7 Renaissance Loggia

An arcaded loggia overlooks the main deck – comparisons to a ship are unavoidable here. The loggia breaks with the military style of most of the building and adds a theatrical element, while the railing and tracery of the balustrade **(left)** are pure Manueline. Balconies on each side of the tower echo the loggia's style.

8 Manueline Twists

Ropes and knots were the main theme for the Manueline masons here. The tracery of some of the balustrades features the near-organic shapes that would be developed in later Manueline buildings.

9 Dungeon

From the tower's vaulted bottom level **(below)** – also used as a dungeon – 17 cannon once covered the approaches to Lisbon.

HOLY NAMESAKE

Belém means Bethlehem – and the name is taken from a chapel dedicated to St Mary of Bethlehem, built in the mid-15th century near the river's edge, in what was then Restelo. This chapel subsequently gave way to the grand Jerónimos church and monastery; the church is still known as Santa Maria de Belém. The name Restelo, for its part, now applies to the area above and behind Belém, a leafy district of fine residences and embassy buildings.

NEED TO KNOW

MAP A6 ■ Avda Brasília ■ 213 620 034 ■ www.torrebelem.gov.pt

Open 10am–5:30pm Tue–Sun (Apr–Sep: to 6:30pm), last adm 5pm; closed 1 Jan, Easter Sun, 1 May, 13 Jun, 24–25 Dec

Adm: €6; senior citizens €3; Youth Card holders €3; under-12s free

■ The tower is at its prettiest in the early morning or late afternoon. Tour groups tend to visit early, so go as late as you can for a quieter visit.

■ Nearby restaurants (including Vela Latina – see p89) often fill up quickly; if you can't find a table, cross the railway line by the footbridge and walk to the nearby Centro Cultural de Belém. Este Oeste, the restaurant here, has great food and a terrace.

10 Armillary Spheres

The armillary spheres carved above the loggia were instruments for showing the motion of the stars around the earth. They became a symbol of Portugal, and still feature on the national flag.

Following pages The cloister of the Sé de Lisboa

TOP 10 ⭐ Museu Nacional do Azulejo

Ceramic tiles, or *azulejos*, are a distinctive aspect of Portuguese culture, featuring in contexts both ordinary and sacred. The art of making them is a Moorish inheritance, much adapted – most noticeably in the addition of human figures, which Islam forbids. This museum dedicated to tiles is enjoyable both for the excellent displays and for its beautiful setting, a 16th-century convent transformed over the centuries to include some of the city's prettiest cloisters and one of its most richly decorated churches.

Lisbon Panel ①
This vast tiled panorama of Lisbon **(right)**, 23 m (75 ft) in length, is a captivating depiction of the city's waterfront as it looked in about 1740, before the great earthquake. It was transferred here from one of the city's palaces.

② Manueline Cloister
This small but stunning cloister **(above)** is one of the few surviving features of the original convent of Madre de Deus. This is the Manueline style at its most restrained. The geometrical wall tiles were added in the 19th century.

③ Nossa Senhora da Vida Altarpiece
Almost 5 m (16 ft) square and containing over 1,000 tiles, this 16th-century Renaissance altarpiece is the work of Marçal de Matos. It depicts the *Adoration of the Shepherds*, flanked by St Luke and St John.

④ Tile-Making Exhibit
Step-by-step exhibits on tile-making, from a lump of clay to final glazing, illuminate how the medium combines the practical and decorative.

⑤ Renaissance Cloister
Part of the first major alteration to the convent in the 16th century, this airy, two-level cloister is the work of Diogo de Torralva. Glassed in to protect visitors and the collection from the weather, it is the light heart of the building.

⑥ Temporary Exhibitions
The ground and first floors have temporary exhibitions on subjects like contemporary tile art, an important art form in Portugal.

7 Moorish Tiles

With their attractive geometric patterns, varied colour palettes and glazing techniques, Moorish tiles **(left)** continue to inspire tile-makers and home decorators alike.

8 Shop

Numerous quality reproductions of classic tile designs are available, as well as modern tiles and other gifts.

A NOD FROM THE 19TH CENTURY

When the southern façade of the church was restored in the late 19th century, the architect used as his model a painting now in the Museu de Arte Antiga *(see pp18–19)*. This shows the convent and church as they looked in the early 16th century. Indoors, the quest for authenticity was less zealous. In one of the cloisters, 19th-century restorers have left a potent symbol of their own era: an image of a steam locomotive has been incorporated into one of the upper-level capitals.

Key to Floorplan
- Second floor
- First floor
- Ground floor

Floorplan of Museu Nacional do Azulejo

9 Cafeteria and Winter Garden

Suitably tiled with food-related motifs, the museum cafeteria is worth a stop for coffee or a light lunch. The courtyard is partly covered and forms a winter garden.

NEED TO KNOW

MAP C2 ▪ Rua da Madre de Deus 4 ▪ 218 100 340

Open 10am–1pm & 2–6pm Tue–Sun; closed 1 Jan, Easter Sun, 1 May, 13 Jun, 24 & 25 Dec

Adm: €5; senior citizens €2.50; Youth Card holders €2.50; under-12s free

▪ The rather awkward location of the Tile Museum can be turned into an asset if you combine it with a visit to Parque das Nações *(see pp20–21)*, a trip to the Panteão Nacional *(see p40)*, or lunch at D'Avis *(see p67)*.

▪ The best place for a drink is the museum's cafeteria; otherwise, head for Alfama and Graça *(see p66)*.

10 Madre de Deus Church

The magnificent barrel-vaulted convent church **(above)**, packed with paintings, is the result of three centuries of construction and decoration. Its layout dates from the 16th century; the tile panels and gilt woodwork are 17th- and 18th-century.

TOP 10 ⭐ Palácio Nacional de Queluz

Queluz is like a miniature Versailles – an exquisite Rococo palace with formal gardens and parkland, just 15 minutes from central Lisbon. Prince Pedro, younger son of Dom João V, had it built as a summer palace in 1747–52. Thirteen years later, when he married his niece, the future Dona Maria I, he commissioned extensions from the French architect Jean-Baptiste Robillon, in order to make it the permanent royal residence. Queluz had a brief golden era before the royal family fled to Brazil after Napoleon's invasion in 1807.

1 Robillon Pavilion

This impressive building **(above)**, replete with windows, balustrades and pillars, is a bit too fussy for purists. It was designed by the French architect Robillon.

2 Gardens

A pair of formal gardens – the Hanging Garden **(above)** and Malta Garden – occupy the space between the palace's two asymmetric wings. Laid out by Robillon, they are adorned with fountains, statues and topiary.

3 Sala dos Embaixadores

The magnificent Ambassadors' Room was used for diplomatic audiences, and is opulently decorated with stuccowork and painted and gilded carved woodwork. Concerts were also held in these grand surroundings and the *trompe l'oeil* ceiling depicts the royal family at such an event.

NEED TO KNOW

MAP A2 ▪ Largo do Palácio ▪ 219 237 300 ▪ www.parquesdes intra.pt

Open Palace: 9am–6pm daily (Gardens: to 6:30pm); closed 1 Jan, 25 Dec

Adm: €10; senior citizens €8.50; children 6–17 €8.50; under-6s free; gardens only €5

▪ An early-morning visit to Queluz can be combined with a trip to Sintra (see pp32–3).

▪ The terrace at the Pousada is the best place for a drink – unless you are lucky enough to have an invitation to an event in the palace itself.

7 Corredor das Mangas

The hallway linking the old and newer parts of Queluz was named for the glass sleeves *(mangas)* of its candles. Painted wall tiles **(left)** give it its other name, the *Corredor dos Azulejos*.

4 Throne Room

Competing in grandeur with the Sala dos Embaixadores, the dome-ceilinged Throne Room also served as the palace's ballroom, church and theatre.

THE PIOUS QUEEN

Dona Maria I, was the first undisputed Queen regnant of Portugal and the first monarch of Brazil. She was a noteworthy ruler but after the death of her son she suffered with poor mental health. In 1807, she was exiled to Brazil with her younger son to escape the invasion of Portugal led by the French Emperor Napoleon.

8 Cozinha Velha and Pousada Dona Maria I

The old palace kitchens have long housed the fine Cozinha Velha restaurant. A drink on the terrace of the newer Pousada Dona Maria I, in the former quarters of the Royal Guard, is as close as you'll get to living at Queluz.

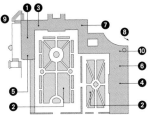

Plan of Palácio Nacional de Queluz

9 Lion Staircase

This beautiful staircase links the lower parkland to the palace. It is flanked by an arcaded gallery with a cascade flowing into a tiled canal; the royal family went boating here.

10 Chapel

The first room to be completed in 1752, the chapel also held concerts, some by Dona Maria I's own chamber orchestra. It is thought that she and her sisters painted some of the wall panels.

5 Don Quixote Chamber

The inlaid circular-pattern floor and domed ceiling make this square room seem round. It is named for its painted scenes from *Don Quixote*.

6 Music Room

The Music Room **(right)** was used for concerts and even opera performances, and doubled as a venue for important christenings. It still serves as a concert venue.

TOP 10 ⭐ Museu Calouste Gulbenkian

Based on the private collections of Calouste Gulbenkian, this museum features the Founder's Collection, which spans over 4,000 years of art history, and is a part of the Gulbenkian Foundation. Internationally recognized for its quality, the museum is part of a complex that houses the headquarters of the Calouste Gulbenkian Foundation, a concert hall and auditoria, an art library and a park. The Foundation also features the Modern Collection, established after the death of Gulbenkian, which is housed in another building within the complex.

1 3rd Dynasty Egyptian Bowl

Found in a tomb north of Thebes, this elegant alabaster bowl was modelled on an everyday ointment bowl. The ancient Egyptians adorned tombs with copies of everyday objects made from noble materials. This one is 4,000 years old.

2 Ancient Greek Vase

This 5th-century BC wide-rimmed terracotta vase **(right)** is decorated with mythological motifs: the abduction of Phoebe and Hilaira by Castor and Pollux, and a bacchanalian scene.

4 Diana Statue

A graceful marble statue by the French sculptor Jean-Antoine Houdon, dating from 1780, is unusual for the era in that it depicts the goddess in movement, and completely naked. It belonged to Catherine the Great of Russia and was exhibited at the Hermitage, where its nudity caused quite a scandal.

3 St Catherine and St Joseph

Two paintings by the 15th-century Flemish master Rogier van der Weyden are believed to be parts of an altarpiece; a third element is in London's National Gallery. The female **(above)** is thought to be Catherine of Alexandria.

5 Lalique Collection

Gulbenkian was a close friend of the French Art Nouveau jeweller René Lalique and bought a great number of his graceful pieces, many on show in this part of the museum.

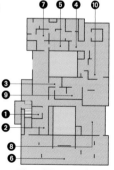

Plan of Museu Calouste Gulbenkian

6 Eastern Islamic Art

This large gallery displays a wide-ranging collection of manuscripts, carpets, textiles, ceramics **(above)** and other objects from Turkey, Syria, the Caucasus (including Armenia), Persia and India.

7 Boy Blowing Bubbles

Édouard Manet's 1867 painting **(right)** is not just a version of the popular allegory on the transience of life and art, but a deftly painted portrait of Léon-Édouard Koëlla, stepson of the artist.

9 Portrait of an Old Man

This engaging *chiaroscuro* portrait of a bearded man is an example of Rembrandt's preoccupation with ageing. The gaze is tired, and the large hands intricately lined. Nothing is known about the model.

8 Yuan Dynasty Stem Cup

This blue-glazed piece, dating from an earlier period (1279–1368) than most of the Far Eastern collection, is decorated with delicate reliefs of Taoist figures under bamboo leaves.

NEED TO KNOW

MAP F1 ■ Avenida de Berna 45A ■ 217 823 000 ■ www. gulbenkian.pt/museu

Open 10am–6pm Wed–Mon; closed 1 Jan, Easter Sun, 1 May, 24–25 Dec

Adm: €10 (for both the Collections); 13–29 years and senior citizens €5; under-12s free; free on Sun after 2pm

■ The Modern Collection (closed for renovation until 2023) comprises of contemporary Portuguese art, and stages frequent temporary shows.

■ There are good cafés at both the Collections.

10 Louis XV and XVI Furniture

Considered ostentatious by some, the 18th-century French pieces **(above)** in the decorative art collection fascinate for their materials and craftsmanship. Highlights include a Louis XV chest inlaid with lacquer panels, gold leaf, mother-of-pearl, bronze and ebony; and a table with a shelf that flips over to reveal a mirror.

TOP 10 ⭐ Sintra

Recognized in 1995 as a UNESCO World Heritage Site, Sintra was the summer residence for Portuguese kings from the 13th to the late 19th centuries. It still possesses many of the classic qualities of a hill retreat: a cooler climate than the city, ample greenery and an atmosphere conducive to romantic whims. The old town is pretty but crowded, while the surrounding landscapes and sights are an essential part of any visit.

Quinta da Regaleira ④

This lavish palace **(right)** looms on a steep bend in the old road to Sintra. It was built around 1900 for António Augusto Carvalho Monteiro, an eccentric millionaire who also owned Peninha *(see p104)*. He was a bibliophile and keen dabbler in alchemy and other esoteric subjects.

① Monserrate

A fantastic Moorish-style palace **(above)** dominates the gardens of Monserrate, which were laid out by English residents.

⑤ São Pedro Market

Antiques are a feature of the lively market held in the suburb of São Pedro on the second and fourth Sundays of each month.

⑥ Palácio de Seteais

Built in 1787, Seteais (now a hotel) got its Neo-Classical façade later. It's best to visit well dressed, for tea or a meal.

② Palácio Nacional da Pena

Dom Fernando II, Dona Maria II's German-born king consort, had this fabulous toyland palace built in the mid-19th century. The work of a lively imagination, it exhibits his eclectic tastes, and is preserved as it was when the royal family lived there **(above)**.

③ Parque da Pena

Filled with beautiful trees and shrubs, the park around the Palácio da Pena is another of Dom Fernando II's contributions to Sintra's magic. It contains the chalet he had built for his second wife, Elise Hensler, an American opera singer.

Map of Sintra

9 Palácio Nacional de Sintra

Twin conical chimneys mark the former royal palace **(left)**. Begun in the 14th century and extended in the 16th, it is a captivating mix of styles from Moorish to Renaissance.

THE ARTIST KING

Ferdinand Saxe-Coburg-Gotha was known in Portugal as Dom Fernando II, the "artist" king. Like his cousin Prince Albert, who married the English Queen Victoria, he loved art, nature and the new inventions of the time. He was himself a water-colour painter. Ferdinand adopted his new country and devoted his life to patronizing the arts. His lifelong dream of building the lavish Palace of Pena was achieved in 1885, but he died before it was completed.

10 Centro Cultural Olga Cadaval

Sintra's main cultural venue, a modern centre hosting dance, theatre, concerts and films, was built in 1987, after a fire destroyed much of the Carlos Manuel cinema.

7 Parque da Liberdade

The town park, with its steep paths running among the trees, occupies the valley below the old town.

Castelo dos Mouros 8

This 10th-century castle **(right)** was captured by Afonso Henriques in 1147. Dom Fernando II partially rebuilt it in the 19th century. A chapel, with an exhibition about the castle's history, and a Moorish cistern are inside.

NEED TO KNOW

30 km (18 miles) NW of Lisbon; trains from Lisbon's Rossio and Sete Rios stations

Tourist information: Praça da República 23, Sintra; 219 231 157; www.cm-sintra.pt, www.parquesdesintra.pt.

■ Sintra's romantic and refreshing qualities may be seriously challenged on summer weekends, when tour groups and locals cross paths in the square in front of the Palácio Nacional de Sintra. Go during the week, and avoid midday in summer.

■ Sampling the town's traditional pastries is a must. Queijadas da Sapa (Volta do Duche 12) serves *queijadas* (sweet cheese tarts) while Casa Piriquita (Rua Padarias 1) is famous for its *travesseiros*, a flaky pastry filled with almond and egg-yolk cream.

The Top 10 of Everything

The Tejo river, as seen from the
Torre de Belém

Moments in History

① 138 BC: Roman Occupation

Despite reaching the Iberian Penisula in the second century BC, it took the Romans over half a century to conquer its westernmost parts from groups like the Lusitanians and the Gallaecians. The trading post of Olisipo (Lisbon's Greek name) was occupied in 138 BC.

② 714: Moorish Occupation

Roman Lisbon was invaded first by the Alani from the north, and then by the Visigoths, who ruled from Toledo. The Visigoths were swept from power by Moorish armies crossing into Iberia at the Straits of Gibraltar. Lisbon fell to the Moors in 714.

③ 1147: Reconquest

The Christian reconquest began in the north, where Afonso Henriques founded the Portuguese kingdom – as distinct from the future Spanish kingdom of León – in 1140. His armies took Lisbon following a three-month siege in 1147.

④ 1497: Voyage to India

In the 15th century, Portugal began a period of maritime journeys known as the Age of Discovery. Vasco da Gama's voyage to India started a spice trade that expanded the country's wealth; simultaneously, however, the trade of enslaved people grew, with Portugal playing a signficant role.

Revolt against the Spaniards, 1640

⑤ 1640: Independence from Spain

Spain had usurped the Portuguese throne in 1581, after the death of Dom Sebastião and many of the Portuguese nobility in a north African military campaign. The 1640 coup at Lisbon's royal palace reinstated self-rule and proclaimed the Duke of Bragança king of Portugal.

⑥ 1755: The Great Earthquake

On 1 November 1755, a massive earthquake struck southern Portugal and laid waste to central Lisbon. Three shocks were followed by devastating fires and tidal waves.

An earthquake wrecks Lisbon, 1755

7. 1910: Portugal Becomes a Republic

In 1908, Dom Carlos and his heir were assassinated by republican activists in Terreiro do Paço. The king's surviving son became Dom Manuel II, but abdicated in October 1910 in the face of a republican revolution. The Republic was formalized on 5 October.

8. 1933: The New State

António de Oliveira Salazar, who had been appointed finance minister in the hope that he could solve the country's financial crisis, was asked to form a government in 1932. The following year his new constitution was passed by parliament, in effect making him an authoritarian dictator.

The Carnation Revolution

9. 1974: The Carnation Revolution

Salazar's successor Marcelo Caetano and his government were overthrown by a group of army captains on 25 April. Four men were killed by shots from the headquarters of the PIDE, the political police, as crowds cheered the end of its reign of fear.

10. 1986: European Union Membership

After a few tumultuous years following the 1974 revolution, a stable democracy was established in Portugal. EU membership brought a boost to the economy through both subsidies and foreign investment. In 2007, the Lisbon Treaty was signed in Belém. Portugal was badly hit by the global economic crisis, but has since recovered thanks to investment in tourism.

TOP 10 HISTORICAL FIGURES

António de Oliveira Salazar

1 Afonso Henriques
Having taken control of the countship of Portucale, Afonso was calling himself "Portucalense king" by 1140.

2 Henry the Navigator
Son of Dom João, Prince Henry was the architect of Portugal's early overseas expansion in the 15th century.

3 Gracia Mendes Nasi
Nasi, a noble Jewish woman born in Lisbon, was forced to escape the Inquisition in Portugal and flee to Constantinople. She helped hundreds of Jews seek refuge in Ottoman lands.

4 Marquis of Pombal
Chief minister under Dom José I, Pombal reconstructed the city after the earthquake of 1755, but was later reviled as a despot by Dona Maria I.

5 Eça de Queiroz
The 19th-century chronicler of Lisbon was a member of the Cenáculo, a group of writers who were opposed to the monarchy.

6 Adelaide Cabete
In 1909, this Portuguese feminist helped create the Republican League of Portuguese Women.

7 Amália Rodrigues
Considered the best Portuguese singer of the 20th century, Rodrigues made *fado* famous worldwide with her music tours.

8 António de Oliveira Salazar
Portugal's deceptively low-key dictator was formerly a professor of economics.

9 Mário Soares
The first democratically elected post-revolution prime minister won a second term and, in 1986, became president of Portugal.

10 Sophia de Mello Breyner Andresen
The first Portuguese woman to receive the Prémio Camões in 1999.

🔟 Museums and Galleries

Central panels from *The Panels of St Vincent* (1460s), Nuno Gonçalves

1 Museu Nacional de Arte Antiga

Portugal's national museum houses priceless national and international works, including painting, sculpture, textiles and decorative art. It is sometimes called the Museu das Janelas Verdes due to the building's location in Rua das Janelas Verdes as well as its green windows (see pp18–19).

2 Museu Nacional do Azulejo

Housed in a stunning convent and church, Lisbon's popular *azulejo* museum covers tiles and tile-making comprehensively, and has a pleasant café-restaurant (see pp26–7).

3 Museu do Design e da Moda (MUDE)

MAP M5 ▪ Rua Augusta 24 ▪ 218 171 892 ▪ Closed for restoration ▪ www.mude.pt

MUDE showcases 20th-century design from around the world.

Star exhibits include Eames chairs and dresses from Dior's landmark 1947 New Look collection.

4 Museu Calouste Gulbenkian

The Armenian oil baron and art collector Calouste Gulbenkian could well be the most important person in Portuguese postwar cultural life. His museum is a rare treat, not just because it covers so much in such a manageable way, but also because it has pleasant gardens and a good contemporary arts centre on site (see pp30–31). The centre is closed for renovation until 2023.

5 Galeria 111

MAP C2 ▪ Rua Dr. João Soares 5B ▪ 217 977 418 ▪ Open 10am–7pm Tue–Sat ▪ www.111.pt

Since opening in 1964, this uptown contemporary art gallery has exhibited Portuguese artists, such as Paula Rego, Júlio Pomar and Joana Vasconcelos, as well as international artists.

6 Museu Nacional dos Coches

You might not visit a coach museum if you didn't have a special interest in the subject. But this is one of Lisbon's most popular museums, thanks to its collection of 68 horse-drawn coaches and the connections they create with the past (see p88).

Exhibit at the Museu Nacional dos Coches

7 Zé dos Bois
MAP K4 ■ Rua da Barroca 59
■ 213 430 205 ■ Gallery: 6–10pm
Mon–Sat; Bar: 6pm–2am Mon–Thu
(until 3am Fri & Sat) ■ Adm ■ www.
zedosbois.org

ZDB, as it is also known, has consistently been Lisbon's most inspirational and genuinely "alternative" gallery. It is also a bar and a concert venue.

8 Museu Nacional de Arte Contemporânea do Chiado (MNAC)
Guardian of Portuguese modernity in art, this museum *(see p78)* has a collection extending from the mid-19th century to the 21st century, though the decades after 1950 are less fully covered. There are also temporary exhibitions.

Gallery in the MNAC

9 Lisbon Story Centre
MAP N5 ■ Praça do Comércio
78–81 ■ 211 941 027 ■ Open
10am–7pm daily ■ Adm ■ www.
lisboastorycentre.pt

This museum offers a romp through Lisbon's history, presented in a series of rooms. Each period of time is recreated through models, paintings and multimedia displays, including a 4D version of the 1755 earthquake.

10 Fundação/Museu Arpad Szenes-Vieira da Silva
MAP F3 ■ Praça das Amoreiras 56
■ 213 880 044 ■ Open 10am–6pm
Tue–Sun ■ Adm ■ www.fasvs.pt

This museum is devoted to the work of Portuguese modernist Maria Helena Vieira da Silva and her Hungarian husband, Arpad Szenes.

TOP 10 PORTUGUESE ARTISTS

1 Nuno Gonçalves
Nuno is believed to be the 15th-century painter of *The Panels of St Vincent*, which may contain his self-portrait.

2 Vhils
Alexandre Farto (b 1987), aka Vhils, is a famous Portuguese street artists, known for his carved wall portraits.

3 Josefa de Óbidos
The work of this female painter and engraver (1630–84) falls between the Mannerist and the Baroque styles.

4 Graça Morais
This celebrated visual artist (b 1948) is known for her intense portraits and rural landscapes, some of which are featured at the Gulbenkian.

5 José Malhoa
A naturalistic painter (1855–1933) most famous for creating *O Fado*.

6 Columbano Bordalo Pinheiro
A gifted portraitist, Columbano (1857–1929) painted many of the leading figures of the Republican movement.

7 Júlio Pomar
One of Portugal's most important 20th-century painters, Pomar (b1926–2018) was at odds with the Fascist dictatorship.

8 Paula Rego
Portugal-born Rego (1935–2022) is known for producing prints and paintings based on children's books and Portuguese folk stories.

9 João Cutileiro
Born in Lisbon, this Portuguese sculptor (1937–2020) was renowned for his marble works depicting women's torsos.

10 Joana Vasconcelos
Feminist artist Vasconcelos (b1971) subverts mundane objects, taking them out of their everyday context and transforming them into sculptures.

***O Fado* (1910), José Malhoa**

Churches and Monasteries

1 Mosteiro dos Jerónimos

The country's most significant monument displays the exuberant and Islamic-inspired ornamentation that is a chief characteristic of the Manueline style *(see pp14–15)*.

2 The Sé de Lisboa

Seen at a distance, Lisbon's cathedral can almost conjure up the mosque that preceded it. Up close, the Romanesque building is attractively simple *(see pp16–17)*.

3 Igreja de São Domingos

One of Lisbon's oldest churches is one of its hardiest survivors *(see p69)*. Built in 1242, it was damaged in the earthquakes of 1531 and 1755, and ravaged by fire in 1959. The church was also the seat of the Inquisition, and outside you'll find a modern memorial honouring the Jewish people killed during this dark time..

4 Basílica da Estrela

MAP E4 ■ **Praça da Estrela** ■ Open 9am–1pm & 3–6:45pm Mon–Sun (mass at 7pm daily)

This landmark was built from 1779 to give thanks for the birth of a male heir to Dona Maria I. Sadly, the boy died of smallpox before the church was finished. Inside is the queen's tomb, and a nativity scene with over 500 cork-and-terracotta figures; ask the sacristan to show it to you.

The Baroque Panteão Nacional

5 Panteão Nacional

An unmistakable feature of the city's eastern skyline, this Baroque beauty is famous for having taken 284 years to complete *(see p64)*. Built on a Greek cross plan with rounded arms, the church has similarities to St Peter's Basilica in Rome, although this church is even-sided. Otherwise known as Igreja de Santa Engrácia, the National Pantheon houses cenotaphs to Portuguese notables, including the writer Almeida Garrett and the *fado* singer Amália Rodrigues.

6 São Vicente de Fora

MAP Q3 ■ **Largo de São Vicente 3** ■ Church: 9am–1pm, 2:30–5pm Tue–Sun (until noon Sun); Monastery: 10am–6pm Tue–Sun ■ Adm (monastery)

In 1173, when St Vincent was proclaimed patron saint of Portugal, his relics were moved from the Algarve to the original church on this site. Philip II of Spain had the present Mannerist church built in the early 1600s. In 1885 the refectory was turned into the pantheon of the Bragança royal family.

7 Igreja de Santo António

MAP N4 ■ **Largo de Santo António da Sé** ■ Open 8am–7pm Mon–Fri (8pm Sat & Sun)

Lisbon's patron saint was allegedly born here (as Fernando Bulhões) in the late 12th century. The present Baroque church replaced the one lost

Interior of the Basílica da Estrela

to the 1755 earthquake. Weddings are held here in June – it's thought that St Anthony brings luck to newlyweds.

Igreja de São Roque

Built in the 16th century for the Jesuit order, this church is famous for its opulent interior, with gold leaf covering the beautiful carved detail, particularly the Chapel of St John the Baptist (see p77). Assembled in Rome, in the 1740s, using the most precious material available at that time, including lapis lazuli, agate, alabaster, amethyst, priceless marbles, gold and silver, the chapel was blessed by the pope, then taken apart and sent to Lisbon in three ships.

9 Igreja do Carmo

The late 14th-century church (see p77) and convent of Carmo was one of Lisbon's main places of worship before the roof caved in on All Saints' Day 1755, killing the congregation. The evocative ruin, with its bare Gothic arches, now houses an archaeological museum.

Ruined arches of Igreja do Carmo

10 Igreja da Graça

MAP P2 ■ Largo da Graça
■ Open 9am–12:30pm & 2–5pm Tue–Fri, 9am–12:30pm & 2–5:30pm Sat, 9am–12:30pm & 5–7:30pm Sun
This 1271 Augustinian monastery, rebuilt after the 1755 earthquake, is home to the Senhor dos Passos, a figure of Christ bearing the cross.

TOP 10 MANUELINE GEMS

Jerónimos Cloister

1 Jerónimos Cloister
João de Castilho's cloister (see p14) has the entire arsenal of Manueline features. Take your time here.

2 Torre de Belém
More decorative than defensive today, this tower (see pp22–3) is a perfect example of the Manueline style.

3 South Portal of Jerónimos
This riot of decoration – featuring saints, royals and other symbols – is completely symmetrical (see p14).

4 Nave of Jerónimos
Mixing organic elements with geometry, octagonal piers encrusted with carvings rise up to the web-like vaulting (see p14).

5 Conceição Velha Portal
This Manueline portal (see p26) is the only remnant of the original 16th-century church, which was destroyed in the 1755 earthquake.

6 Portal, Museu do Azulejo
This dates from the 19th century, when the façade was reconstructed from a 16th-century painting (see p27).

7 Manueline Cloister, Museu do Azulejo
This small and restrained cloister (see p26) is a reminder of the building's 16th-century role as a convent.

8 Ermida de São Jerónimo
This simple chapel from 1514 (see p15) gives the Manueline a broader, more contemporary aesthetic.

9 Casa dos Bicos
This 16-century palace combines Italian-style architecture with Manueline windows. It houses the José Saramago Foundation (www.josesaramago.org).

10 Rossio Station
A nostalgic Neo-Manueline look back from 1892, with a hint of parallels to Art Nouveau (see p72).

🔟 City Views

Magnificent view over the Baixa and Castelo de São Jorge

1 Miradouro de Santa Luzia
MAP P4

This romantic viewpoint by the church of Santa Luzia has a pergola with tiled pillars, walls and benches. The veranda has dazzling vistas over the Alfama and across the river, a view shared by the adjacent café.

2 Castelo de São Jorge
MAP N3

The view from under the umbrella pines on the castle's esplanade takes in Alfama, the Baixa, Bairro Alto on the hill opposite, and the river. The light here is particularly appealing in the late afternoon. It is also a great spot from which to watch the sun set.

3 Miradouro de São Pedro de Alcântara
MAP K2

This small garden is one of Lisbon's best-known viewpoints. Bougainvillea tumbles onto the next terrace, a more formal and less accessible garden. The view extends across Restauradores and the Baixa to the Sé de Lisboa and the castle.

4 Miradouro de Santa Catarina
MAP J5

Not just a visual vantage point, this is also a place to meet and hang out. A sculpture of Adamastor, the mythical creature from Camões' epic poem *The Lusiads*, presides over events from a stone plinth. There's a wide view of the river, encompassing the station at Cais do Sodré, the Alcântara docks and the 25 de Abril bridge.

5 Igreja da Graça
MAP P2

The pine-shaded esplanade by the Graça church has a café with a classic view of the lower city, the river and the bridge. Like the castle's viewpoint, this one is best visited in the late afternoon.

6 Elevador de Santa Justa
The best close-up overview of the Baixa and Rossio, with the castle looming above, is to be had from the terrace at the top of the Elevador de Santa Justa *(see p70)*. It is reached via an extremely tight spiral staircase, but the view is definitely worth the climb.

7 Parque Eduardo VII
MAP F2

This park is not the most popular, thanks to its formal plan, steep incline and lack of shade. But climb to the top and the architect's plan makes sense, as Lisbon stretches away from you in an unbroken perspective right down to the river. The sides of the park have a less commanding view but offer more shade.

Parque Eduardo VII's unbroken vista

At the end of summer, bookworms gather in the park for the Feira do Livro, Lisbon's annual book fair.

Miradouro da Senhora do Monte

8 Miradouro da Senhora do Monte
MAP P1

One of the highest vantage points in the city, Our Lady of the Mount (there is a small chapel behind the viewpoint) affords a grand vista that encompasses the castle, the Graça church and the Mouraria quarter, as well as the Tejo estuary, the lower city, midtown Lisbon and the Monsanto park.

9 Jardim do Torel
MAP L1

The Jardim do Torel is a less well known viewpoint, a small garden on a slope overlooking Restauradores and the Avenida da Liberdade. It provides not just a fine view of the city, but a great place for quiet contemplation, too.

10 Arco da Rua Augusta
MAP M5

This impressively ornate arch dominates the north side of Praça do Comércio. It was built as a gateway to the reconstructed city following the 1755 earthquake, with the statues at the top representing Portuguese figures from history. Take a lift and a narrow spiral staircase to the top of the arch for stunning views over downtown Baixa. On the way back down, you can visit the Clock Room, an exhibition space alongside the workings of the original 19th-century clock.

Beaches

1 Caparica Norte
South of Lisbon, the Caparica coast is busiest at its northern end, where you'll find Caparica town, plus an assortment of mid-range hotels, holiday homes, campsites and restaurants.

2 Caparica Centre
Further south, the Caparica beach gets less busy, but has fewer amenities. From June to September the Transpraia train runs from Caparica town to Fonte da Telha, stopping at bars and restaurants en route. The beach at Fonte da Telha is great for families, but note that many facilities are closed out of season.

3 Carcavelos
The broadest and longest beach along the Estoril coast is far enough from Lisbon for clean water and yet close enough for an after-noon outing. Beachside bars and restaurants provide ample opportunity for meals and refreshments. This is an excellent surfing area, and there are a number of surf schools at the beach. Carcavelos is still extremely pleasant out of season.

4 Estoril and Cascais
These beaches get very crowded, as they are mostly short and narrow. Still, the promenade that runs just above them, all the way from Estoril to Cascais, is full of relaxed bars and restaurants, where you can also take in the sun.

Clifftop view of Adraga beach

5 Adraga
Beyond Cabo da Roca, this pretty beach is reached via Almoçageme, off the Sintra road. Sintra's cooler climate prevails in this area. There's just one restaurant, but it is excellent.

6 Guincho
Guincho can provide an eyeful of sand on a windy day, but experienced surfers love it and it is the least developed of all the beaches along the Cascais coast. Beyond the built-up outskirts of Cascais, and with the Sintra hills as a backdrop, Guincho is a magnificent spot, and it draws the crowds on summer weekends. To avoid parking hassles, rent a

The beach and promenade along the coast at Cascais

bicycle in Cascais and ride out on the track that runs alongside the spectacular coast road.

 Grande

With the longest unbroken stretch of sand in the area, Grande is popular with surfers and body-boarders. There are also plenty of bars and restaurants, and one hotel.

 Lagoa de Albufeira and Meco

The southern half of the Caparica coast is accessible only by driving towards Sesimbra. Lagoa de Albufeira is a lagoon popular with kite-surfers. Further south, Meco is backed by a village with restaurants and bars.

Das Maçãs

"Apple Beach" is one of the most family-friendly along the Sintra-Colares coast. There are lots of good seafood restaurants nearby.

Towering cliffs at secluded Ursa

Ursa

Not marked on maps and requiring a steep walk on narrow paths, Ursa is one of the most secluded beaches in the region. Surrounded by towering cliffs, it has no amenities and – as there are no lifeguards here and the waves can be powerful – anything beyond a short dip close to shore is not advisable. The beach is reached along the road to Cabo da Roca, where there is a small sign marked Ursa. Leave your car at the small parking area near this sign.

TOP 10 OUTDOOR ACTIVITIES

Mountain biking in Arrábida

1 Mountain Biking
Lisbon's hills provide ideal terrain for mountain biking. For country biking, head to the tracks around Sintra or Arrábida.

2 Cycling
Cycling is becoming increasingly popular in Lisbon, and bikes can be rented in Cascais and near Belém.

3 Board Sports
Surfing and body-boarding are big along the Estoril and Sintra coasts, as is kite-surfing on the Caparica coast.

4 Fishing
Fishers seem to be all along the river and beaches. Tourists hoping to cast out a line can take organized boat trips off the coast of Cascais.

5 Bird-watching
The Tagus marshlands beyond Alcochete and the Tróia peninsula are rich in bird life almost all year round.

6 Sailing
There are sailing schools in Parque das Nações, Belém and along the Cascais coast. Renting larger craft is possible.

7 Horse Riding
There are a number of *equestre* or *hípico* clubs around Cascais and Sintra, and around Campo Grande in Lisbon.

8 Jogging
The western riverfront is reasonable jogging territory, as is Parque Eduardo VII. Monsanto and the Guincho coast are other options.

9 Walking
For dirt rather than cobbles underfoot, head for Sintra, Arrábida or the area surrounding the Tejo estuary.

10 Roller Skating
Parque das Nações, the Alcântara docks and Belém all have areas suitable for skating.

📑 Off the Beaten Track

The Cristo Rei monument and shrine towers over Lisbon

1 Cristo Rei
Almada ▪ 212 751 000
▪ Open 10am–7pm daily (to 6pm Oct–Mar) ▪ www.cristorei.pt

From his perch on the south side of the river, Christ the King overlooks Lisbon. The 28-m (92-ft) statue on its 82-m (270-ft) pedestal was inaugurated in 1959, in thanks for Portugal's escape from involvement in World War II. Inspired by the famous statue in Rio de Janeiro, it has since become an important site of pilgrimage. Lifts ascend to the platform at the foot of the statue.

2 Almada
The characterful old centre of this city offers fine views back over Lisbon. Take the modern lift, Elevador da Boca do Vento, to the attractive riverside strip of Jardim do Rio.

Prazeres tomb

3 Cacilhas
Enjoy a ferry ride from Cais do Sodré to this little port opposite Lisbon, which is home to some terrific fish restaurants, as well as the *Dom Fernando II e Glória*, a restored 19th-century frigate that is now a museum.

4 Prazeres
MAP D4 ▪ Praça São João Bosco ▪ 218 173 780 ▪ Open 9am–5:30pm daily (Oct–Apr: to 4:30pm) ▪ www.cm-lisboa.pt

Take tram 28 to the end of the line to visit Lisbon's main cemetery, a neatly laid-out village of pristine tombs. This tranquil spot is where some of Lisbon's most important inhabitants have been buried, among some of Iberia's oldest cypress trees.

5 Praça das Amoreiras
MAP E3

Locals like to sit drinking coffee at a kiosk under the trees in this hidden-away square, complete with children's play area. The space is flanked by the arches of the last stretches of the 18th-century Aqueduto das Águas Livres, which brought water to the capital.

An aerial view of Almada city

6 Aqueduto das Águas Livres

If you have a head for heights, you can walk across the top of the most dramatic part of Lisbon's extraordinary aqueduct (see pp86–7). It was built over a decade before the 1755 earthquake – which it survived, continuing to supply water to a shattered city. Head for the section that crosses the Alcântara Valley. Some of the arches here are over 64 m (210 ft) high, and were the tallest stone arches in the world at the time they were built.

7 Palácio das Necessidades

MAP D5 ■ Largo das Necessidades ■ Gardens: 8am–8pm Mon–Fri, 10am–7pm Sat & Sun (Oct–Mar: closes one hour earlier) ■ www.cm-lisboa.pt

This charming 18th-century palace was built by Dom João V and used by Portuguese royals until 1910. It now belongs to the Foreign Ministry. The interior is closed to the public, but the gardens are delightful.

Palácio das Necessidades

8 Lapa

MAP E5

Set on a steep hillside overlooking the Tejo (or Tagus, in English), Lapa is the city's most desirable district. This is an area of lavish villas and mansions occupied by embassies, consulates and the rich. It's a great place to stroll, past tempting cafés and exclusive restaurants.

9 Poço dos Negros Area

MAP F4 ■ Rua do Poço dos Negros/Rua de São Bento/Rua dos Poiais de São Bento

Located between Estrela and Bairro Alto, this area has become one of Lisbon's creative hotspots (see p55). Here you'll find traditional grocery shops such as Mercearia Poço dos Negros alongside modern design stores and trendy cafés such as The Mill and Hello, Kristoff.

10 Barbadinhos Steam Pumping Station

Rua do Alviela 12 ■ **218 100 215** ■ Open 10am–12:30pm & 1:30–5:30pm Tue–Sun ■ Adm ■ www.epal.pt

This fascinating relic of Victorian ingenuity was built in 1880 to pump water from a nearby reservoir up Lisbon's steep hills. It worked non-stop until 1928. The museum also hosts temporary exhibits.

TOP 10 Activities for Children

Interactive exhibits at the Knowledge Pavilion museum

1 Knowledge Pavilion – Ciência Viva

This hands-on science museum (see p21) has intriguing gadgetry to illustrate the fundamental laws of nature, including a bicycle ride on a 6-m- (20-ft-) high wire. Downstairs, the youngest visitors get the chance to don hard hats and help build the Unfinished House.

2 Quinta da Regaleira

Underground tunnels, spiral staircases and hidden tree paths make this 20th-century estate (see p32) a fun maze to explore for kids and adults alike. Follow the steps down the initiation well and don't miss the stepping stones over the water stream. Bring a flashlight as some passages can get pretty dark.

Initiation well, Quinta da Regaleira

3 Oceanário de Lisboa

Opened for the 1998 Lisbon Expo, the Oceanário de Lisboa (see p20) remains the biggest single attraction in Parque das Nações. One of Europe's biggest aquariums, it holds an impressive array of species.

4 Monsanto
MAP B2

Monsanto (see p86) is a pine wood located on the city's western fringes. The Parque Recreativo do Alto da Serafina and Parque Infantil do Alvito are both popular, fenced-off, well-equipped play areas.

5 Quake
MAP B6 ■ Rua Cais de Alfândega Velha 39 ■ Entry at specific time slots between 10am and 7pm ■ https://lisbonquake.com ■ Adm (book tickets online for discounts); free 4–5 yrs

Experience Lisbon's 1755 earthquake at this interactive museum, complete with simulators. Children under four are not admitted.

6 Roller Skating, Ice Skating and Skateboarding

There are several places in Lisbon with ramps and rinks for roller skating and skateboarding. One of the best is by the Vasco da Gama bridge in Parque das

Nações *(see p20)*. In winter, an outdoor ice rink is erected in Parque Eduardo VII *(see p95)*.

Swimming Pools

Many hotels have outdoor pools. The Clube Nacional de Natação has a complex with indoor and outdoor pools at Rua de São Bento 209, or try the Piscina do Oriente at Rua Câmara Reis in east Lisbon.

8 Museu da Electricidade

MAP B6 ■ Avenida de Brasilia ■ Open 10am–7pm Wed–Mon

Located on Lisbon's waterfront, the Electricity Museum, which is a part of the MAAT *(see p88)*, includes a section where children can play and learn.

Museu da Electricidade exhibit

9 Beaches

The Atlantic is not the safest water for young ones to play in. Low tide is an advisable time for building sand castles and paddling in pools left by the receding sea. Some of the beaches along the Cascais coast *(see p44)* are more protected; alternatively head for Portinho de Arrábida or Tróia *(see pp58–9)*.

10 Museu Nacional de História Natural e da Ciência

MAP J2 ■ Rua da Escola Politécnica 58 ■ Open 10am–5pm Tue–Sun (Gardens: until 8pm in summer) ■ Adm

Housed in the grand setting of the old Polytechnic, this science and natural history museum by the Jardim Botânico *(see pp84–5)* has an engaging hands-on exhibit illustrating the basic principles of physics.

TOP 10 FAMILY-FRIENDLY RESTAURANTS

Nosolo Itália treats

1 Nosolo Itália
A tempting array of pizzas, pastas and ice creams are served on a large outdoor terrace *(see p89)*.

2 Mercado da Ribeira
Avenida 24 de Julho ■ www. timeoutmarket.com
With 24 restaurants under one roof, there is something for all ages.

3 Casanova
A popular quay-side pizzeria with a safe veranda; kids can watch the chef at work *(see p67)*.

4 Café Buenos Aires
The steps outside are traffic-free; inside, the vibe is friendly *(see p83)*.

5 Psi
The pretty gardens surrounding this restaurant are perfect for children to play in *(see p99)*.

6 Chapitô a Mesa
Costa do Castelo 7 ■ 218 875 077
Part of a popular circus school, this restaurant offers amazing views and a delightful menu.

7 APF Lisboa
MAP E4 ■ Rua da Trinas 67A ■ 211 947 477
This family-friendly space offers a playground and a restaurant with a kids menu.

8 Restaurants at Doca de Santo Amaro
Doca de Santo Amaro
Facing a marina, these family-friendly restaurants have outdoor tables.

9 Restaurants in Parque das Nações
Parque das Nações
Choices range from food courts to riverside terraces and steak houses.

10 Restaurants along Rua Vieira Portuense, Belém
This is a short street of outdoor restaurants overlooking the Jardim de Belém *(see p88)*.

Bars and Nightclubs

Lisboa Rio

This stylish Mediterranean restaurant and bar, with a beautiful terrace overlooking the dock, transforms into a swanky nightclub at weekends. With both resident and guest DJs from all over the world, there is lively music and entertainment *(see p90)*.

2 Cais do Gás

MAP F5 ■ www.caisdogas.com

Old warehouses along Lisbon's riverfront have been converted into bars and clubs. Classics like Jamaica and Tokyo moved here from Pink Street, joining others like Titanic Sur Mer, with its live acts, and B.Leza *(see p90)*, famous for its afro tunes.

3 Hot Clube

For a night of jazz, pop by the Hot Clube *(see p98)*, an intimate concert venue near Avenida da Liberdade. Open since the 1940s, it's among the oldest jazz clubs in Europe, hosting Portuguese and international artists.

4 Lux

MAP R3 ■ Cais da Pedra, Avenida Infante Dom Henrique

Located by the harbour and housed in a former warehouse, Lux is consi-

Clubgoers at Lux

A refreshing pint of beer

dered Lisbon's most stylish and varied nightclub. With a downstairs dance floor, an upstairs bar and dance area, a rooftop terrace, retro decor and a string of hot DJs, it lives up to the hype.

5 Bar Lounge

Resident disc-spinner Mário Valente has been working to enrich Bar Lounge's eclectic mix of indie and electronic pop and rock since the early noughties. Located down an alley, Bar Lounge has a full programme of live bands that, combined with a relaxed atmosphere, has earned it a loyal following *(see p90)*.

6 Zé dos Bois

This cultural institution *(see p39)* is a bar, art gallery and concert venue. It plays mostly alternative and electronic music promoting both Portuguese and international acts. See its website for the latest gigs.

7 Incógnito

MAP F4 ■ Rua dos Poiais de São Bento 37

This veteran of the early 1990s has kept on doing what it does best and draws a mostly low-profile crowd. Somewhere between a bar and a club, it accommodates both chill-out areas and a dance floor. The music is a mixed bag, with recent dance sounds on weeknights and a broader spectrum at weekends.

8 Ministerium

MAP G5 ■ Terreiro do Paço, Ala Nascente 72–73

This stylish nightclub, with a large dance floor and bar, has one of the best locations in town, plus music from some of the world's top DJs. Comfortable chairs have been set up in corners for an occasional retreat from the music, which veers towards techno and electronica. Open only on Fridays and Saturdays.

Lively Rua Nova do Carvalho

9 Rua Nova do Carvalho (Pink Street)

MAP K6

Once the sort of street to avoid after dark, this has now been cleaned up and rebranded as "Pink Street", thanks to the alarming colour of the road. The result: one of the hippest streets in which to spend the evening. Old dance clubs such as Roterdão Club are still to be found, alongside trendy bars such as Povo, Sol e Pesca and the club/music venue Musicbox.

10 Dock's Club

MAP D5 ■ Rua da Cintura do Porto ■ Tue–Sun

A well-established dance venue on West Lisbon's waterfront, Dock's Club has a ladies' night every Tuesday. The club hosts live music on Fridays, and the popular Saturday Night Fever takes place the following night.

TOP 10 FADO VENUES

Parreirinha de Alfama

1 Parreirinha de Alfama
Beco do Espírito Santo 1 ■ 218 868 209
A traditional venue set up by the famous singer Argentina Santos.

2 Clube de Fado
Rua de São João da Praça 94
■ 218 852 704
This Alfama *fado* venue hosts fadistas like Maria Ana Bobone.

3 Senhor Vinho
Rua do Meio à Lapa 18 ■ 213 972 681
Quality and style characterize the singing at this expensive restaurant.

4 Timpanas
Rua Gilberto Rola 24 ■ 213 906 655
Timpanas offers a superb dinner show with first-class *fado*.

5 Tasca do Chico
Rua do Diário de Notícias 39
■ 961 339 696
The place to see gritty *fado vadio*: amateur impromptu performances.

6 Café Luso
Travessa da Queimada 10
■ 213 422 281
Offering first-class *fado* and fine food in the Bairro Alto since the 1920s.

7 Sr Fado
Rua dos Remédios 176 ■ 914 431 971
Warm and friendly venue with some of the best *fado* performers in town.

8 A Severa
Rua das Gáveas 51 ■ 213 428 314
An atmospheric venue named after the famous 19th-century *fadista*.

9 Fado em Si
Rua de São João da Praça 18
■ 211 387 418
Set in an old palace, which features one of Lisbon's original walls.

10 O Faia
Rua da Barroca 54 ■ 213 426 742
One of Bairro Alto's larger venues, with good music and expensive food.

🔟 Restaurants

Cosy setting inside Alma

the favourites. Try the *prego* (a juicy steak sandwich) which is a popular dessert here. Make sure to arrive early or get ready to queue.

④ A Travessa
In the grand surroundings of an old convent (shared with private residents and a puppet museum), this welcoming restaurant *(see p91)* feels like it could be in a provincial town. The food, though, is cosmo-politan, successfully mixing Portuguese, Belgian and French influences, all prepared with fresh seasonal ingredients.

① Alma
Run by chef Henrique Sá Pessoa, this two-Michelin-star restaurant *(see p83)* is located in the Chiado district. The menu is inspired from his travels around the world, combining traditional Portuguese cuisine with Asian flavours. Opt for the "Alma" degus-tation menu featuring the Chef's classics, or the "Costa a Costa" for the best of Portuguese seafood. You can also order à la carte.

⑤ Belcanto
Warm wooden floors and arched ceilings set the scene for this fine dining restaurant *(see p83)* in the heart of Chiado. Chef José Avillez runs many venues in Lisbon, including a self-contained neighbourhood called Bairro do Avillez, but this is his two Michelin-starred establishment. The tasting menus offer a creative take on classic Portuguese cuisine. The Chef's Table option allows guests to sit in the kitchen and observe the preparation up close.

② Real Fábrica
MAP F3 ■ Rua da Escola Politécnica 275 ■ 213 852 090 ■ Closed Sun ■ €
This well-established restaurant, located just off Largo do Rato, is spread across two floors. They serve traditional Portuguese cuisine, with the grilled fish being a speciality. The restaurant also offers homemade desserts and an extensive wine list.

⑥ Casa do Alentejo
Overlooking a Moorish-style interior courtyard, this "embassy of the Alentejo region" is one of Lisbon's most memorable dining locations

③ Cervejaria Ramiro
MAP N1 ■ Avenida Almirante Reis 1 ■ 218 851 024 ■ Closed Mon ■ €€€
Open since 1956, Ramiro is a seafood lover's paradise. Lobster, stuffed crab and giant tiger prawns are among

Tiled interior at Casa do Alentejo

(see p75). Try traditional dishes like *açorda* (bread soup) or order a selection of Portuguese sausages. On rare occasions, an Alentejan choir can be heard practising in an adjoining room.

7 Eleven

A modernist window box at the top of Parque Eduardo VII (see p43) is the setting for Lisbon's most sophisticated contemporary restaurant (see p99). Joachim Koerper is the chef behind the meticulously prepared food. Drapes, low lights and soft music serve to enhance the ambience.

Beautifully presented food at Eleven

8 Taberna Sal Grosso

Sample hearty dishes and local craft beer at this cosy tavern (see p67) in Alfama. For delicious fresh fish, you can ask about the catch of the week.

9 Solar dos Presuntos

MAP L2 ■ Rua das Portas de Santo Antão 150 ■ 213 424 253 ■ Closed Sun ■ €€€

A traditional restaurant known for its mouthwatering *presunto* (cured ham) as well as other superb meat and seafood dishes. It also has a good selection of wines. Reservations are recommended.

10 Zé da Mouraria 2

MAP G3 ■ Rua Gomes Freire 60 ■ 216 084 695 ■ Closed Sun ■ €€

This restaurant is known especially for its roasted codfish and steak. The portions served here are big enough to share.

TOP 10 CAFÉS AND PASTELARIAS

Confeitaria Nacional

1 Confeitaria Nacional
There are always queues for the pastries at this Lisbon institution – a sure sign of quality (see p74).

2 Antiga Confeitaria de Belém
The birthplace of the original *pastel de nata* is a must for pastry enthusiasts.

3 Bénard
For cakes, this is a much better option than the famous but crowded A Brasileira next door (see p81).

4 Manteigaria
Rua do Loreto 2
Head to this bakery, opposite Largo do Camões (see p79), for *pastéis de nata*.

5 Heim Café
Rua Santos-O-Velho 2-4
A few steps from the Museu de Arte Antiga (see p86) is this trendy brunch spot serving avocado toasts and coffee.

6 Café Mexicana
This classic Lisbon café-restaurant and social club is big and busy (see p99).

7 Pastelaria Versailles
Dream your way back to a time before fast food in this unreformed relic of old Lisbon (see p99).

8 Panificação Mecânica
Rua Silva Carvalho 209–25
This bakery and pastry shop, named after its early use of machinery, is an Art Nouveau jewel serving tasty treats.

9 Pão de Canela
Praça das Flores 27
This pleasant café has a terrace on quaint Praça das Flores. Children can play safely nearby.

10 A Brasileira
Once the haunt of Lisbon's literary elite, this café is now one of the city's most famous (see p81).

For a key to restaurant price ranges see p67

Shopping Districts

① Baixa
MAP M4–5

The charm of the Baixa lies with its courteous shopkeepers, some of whom still stand behind wooden counters and do sums on bits of paper. For all that, the pedestrianized Rua Augusta is lined with modern chains.

Shop-lined Rua Augusta, Baixa

② Chiado
MAP L4

Traditionally the quarter with Lisbon's most elegant shops, the Chiado is now the city's most varied shopping area. It mixes quiet streets with lively squares and sheet-music suppliers with street-cred fashion boutiques.

③ Avenidas Guerra Junqueiro/Roma
MAP G1

Head to Avenida Guerra Junqueiro and adjacent Avenida de Roma for good clothes shops and cafés – and pay a visit to the Museu Rafael Bordalo Pinheiro *(see p98)*. There is also a shopping complex nearby with several boutiques and delicatessens.

④ Avenida da Liberdade
MAP F3

Lisbon's main avenue, rising from the Baixa to the Parque Eduardo VII, has become the country's prime slice of real estate. It is lined with shops owned by upmarket designer brands, including Cartier, Gucci, Armani, Hugo Boss and Prada.

⑤ Campo de Ourique/Amoreiras
MAP E3

Gentrification proceeds at a gentle pace in Campo de Ourique. The grid street plan makes for lots of corner bakeries, cafés and small shops. Nearby, the brash Amoreiras Towers, Lisbon's first modern shopping centre, tempts shoppers.

⑥ Rua de São Bento/Rua da Escola Politécnica
MAP F4

Rua de São Bento is a mini-district specializing in antiques and second-hand shops. It's a short hop to pleasant Praça das Flores for a coffee under the trees, and then an uphill walk to Rua da Escola Politécnica, and a cluster of more expensive antiques shops.

⑦ Fresh Food Markets
MAP K6, E3, F2

Prices at Lisbon's food markets may not be lower than in the supermarkets, but the produce is often fresher and the experience is much more rewarding. Among the best are Mercado da Ribeira, opposite Cais do Sodré station; Mercado de Campo de Ourique, in west Lisbon; and Mercado 31 de Janeiro, opposite the DoubleTree by Hilton hotel on Rua Engenheiro Vieira da Silva.

Mercado da Ribeira

Bairro Alto clothes shop

8 Bairro Alto
MAP K3–4

Like the big shopping centres, Bairro Alto offers night-time shopping, but in a much cooler setting, and with the option of sipping a drink as you shop. Some stores seem ineffably trendy, but Bairro Alto is a nursery for Portuguese fashion and design.

9 Poço dos Negros Area
MAP R3

Running along the 28 tram line, this is one of the city's creative corners (see p47). Here local design shops and trendy cafés mix with traditional Portuguese restaurants and a tea store which sells local blends like the Lisbon Breakfast.

Feira da Ladra bargains

10 Feira da Ladra
MAP Q2 ■ Campo de Santa Clara ■ Open 9am–6pm Tue & Sat

Lisbon's Thieves' Market sells quirky items such as beautiful brass taps that won't fit any known plumbing system. As with most flea markets, it's all about the sights and sounds, the people and the haggling.

TOP 10 THINGS TO BUY

1 Ceramics
Portuguese ceramics extend from tiles to pottery, and from rustic to twee.

2 Embroidery
Bordados are delicate, but long-lasting, old-world table linen.

3 Cork items
Portugal is the world's biggest exporter of cork. Local artisans use this sustainable material to make a variety of objects, including wallets, umbrellas and shoes.

4 Shoes
Fewer shoes are made in Portugal these days, but those that are tend to be of a very high quality.

5 Tea
Discover unique local tea blends at the Companhia Portugueza do Chá.

6 Beauty Supplies
Find delightful-smelling soaps wrapped in stunning vintage-inspired packaging at Claus Porto.

7 Cheese
Choose from runny Serra ewe's milk cheeses, delicious Serpa and Azeitão, peppery Castelo Branco and excellent hard and soft goat's cheeses.

8 Hams and Smoked Meats
The best *presunto* (cured ham) is from the north, but the Alentejan ham of the Ibérico pig is arguably better. Taste first, and decide for yourself.

9 Preserved Foods
Sardines and other tinned fish, olives, olive oil, *massa de pimentão* (red-pepper paste) and chilli sauce are all superb and readily available.

10 Wine
A wisely spent €5 will get you a truly good wine; €20 an unforgettable one. The wide choice is a pleasant surprise.

Wine shop

TOP10 Lisbon for Free

Seafront promenade at Cascais

1 Cascais Coast

Lisbon is close to some fantastic stretches of beach. Head to Estoril and you can walk up the seafront promenade to Cascais, past several sandy beaches *(see p101)*.

2 Museu do Dinheiro

MAP M5 ■ Largo de S. Julião
■ 213 213 240 ■ Open 10am–6pm Wed–Sun ■ www.museudodinheiro.pt

The Money Museum portrays the evolution of Portugal's various currencies over the centuries. One of the highlights of the museum is a rare portion of the city's original King Dinis Wall in the crypt of an old church.

3 Riverside Walk

MAP D6–A6

The riverside is largely traffic-free from the Doca de Santo Amaro to the Torre de Belém, making for a lovely stroll past the dramatic Ponte 25 de Abril and Belém's monuments.

The riverside Torre de Belém

4 Jerónimos Church

MAP B6 ■ Praça do Império
■ 213 620 034

The church of Santa Maria de Belém, built to commemorate Vasco da Gama's voyage to India over 500 years ago, is Portugal's most striking example of Manueline architecture and also an integral part of Mosteiro dos Jerónimos *(see pp14–15)*.

5 Núcleo Arqueológico da Rua dos Correeiros

Phone ahead to book a fascinating free guided tour that takes you below the Millennium BCP bank in Baixa *(see p70)*. Builders uncovered ancient remains here while working on the bank in the 1990s, and excavations have revealed Roman fish-preserving tanks, Moorish ceramics and Christian graves.

Artifacts at the Núcleo Arqueológico

6 Jardim Gulbenkian

The Calouste Gulbenkian's *(see pp30–31)* modernist gardens offer a quiet respite from the city's bustle. Ducks paddle around the large central pond, while turtles hide in little streams. It's a favourite spot for residents who come here for a reading break, a family picnic, or to catch the latest exhibit at the museums nearby.

7 Festival for Santo António

MAP H4 ■ Alfama

On 12–13 June, Lisbon celebrates its main saint's day. There are free daytime parades and most districts

Parade at the Santo António festival

have evening street parties with food stalls and dancing. The Alfama is the best place to head if you want to join in the festivities.

 Jardim da Estrela
MAP E4 ▪ Praça da Estrela

Nestling in the shadow of the basilica, the well-maintained Estrela Gardens in the western part of the city, are very popular with locals. There's a small lake and a bandstand set in the middle of neat flower beds, statues and pleasant walkways. Visitors can also relax at the open-air cafés which offer various options for snacks.

9 Feira da Ladra

Lisbon's rambling flea market is as good for people-watching as it is for finding the odd bargain among a panoply of clothes, antiques, crafts and people's cast-offs. Get there when the market opens to spot the most interesting characters and items.

10 Rua Augusta

The broad, pedestrianized main street through the Baixa usually offers plenty of free entertainment, from living statues to mime artists. Look out for the triumphal arch at the end of the street *(see p69)*.

TOP 10 BUDGET TIPS

1 You can explore all of central Lisbon on foot. Make sure you have sturdy shoes to negotiate its many hills.

2 Locals spend whole days at the giant shopping centres such as Amoreiras *(see p54)*, Centro Colombo *(see p98)* or Centro Vasco da Gama in the Parque das Nações *(see pp20–21)*. Along with shops and supermarkets, they are home to some of the city's least expensive cafés and fast-food outlets.

3 The Bilhete Diário, a one-day travel pass (€10.70), allows unlimited access to buses, trains, the metro and trams. There is also a 24-hour train only pass (€6).

4 The Lisboa Card (€21 for one day, €35 for two days, €44 for three days), available from tourist offices, allows free travel on public transport and admission to 37 major sights around the city.

5 Take the cheaper passenger ferry from Cais do Sodré to Cacilhas across the Tejo; it's a shorter ride than a boat trip, but the views are just as good.

6 Check for free festivals, concerts or events on the city's listings website, www.agendalx.pt.

7 Take advantage of the good-value set meals in cafés and restaurants.

8 It's normal to be offered an array of starters when you sit down in a restaurant, but you'll pay for anything you eat. Politely decline anything you don't want.

9 You'll save money by ordering a drink from the counter or bar of a café rather than taking a seat and being served by a waiter.

10 There are inexpensive bike hire outfits on the riverfront at Belém and in Cascais; cycling is the best way to explore these relatively flat districts.

Cycling in Lisbon's streets

🔟 Excursions

1 Sintra Hills
The romantic beauty of Sintra (see pp32–3) and its palaces – the crumbling walls veiled with moss, the views, the winding roads under dense canopies of leaves – all combine to make a visit to the Sintra hills a magical experience.

2 Serra da Arrábida
This limestone massif, about 40 minutes south of Lisbon by car, provides Portugal with its Mediterranean-like scenery – calm, blue-green waters and dramatic cliffs. Head for Portinho da Arrábida, and stop frequently to admire the views as you get close.

3 Alcácer do Sal
The ancient town of Alcácer do Sal (al-kasr from the Arabic for castle, and do sal from its trade in salt) sits peacefully on the north bank of the River Sado. Here you can enjoy the views from the 6th-century castle (now a pousada) and relax in the pleasant cafés along the riverside promenade.

4 Palmela and Azeitão
The main sight in Palmela is its hilltop castle, now an elegant pousada, which is open to passing visitors. Vila Fresca de Azeitão and Vila Nogueira de Azeitão are neighbouring towns at the heart of Palmela wine country.

Flamingoes on the Tróia peninsula

5 Setúbal and Tróia
The port town of Setúbal is prosaic, but it is home to the Igreja de Jesus, the first and perhaps most distinctive example of the Manueline style. People and cars are ferried across the mouth of the Sado river to the Tróia peninsula, which has excellent beaches extending south, and its estuary side is a haven for birds.

6 Tejo Estuary
Referred to in English as the Tagus, the estuary is accessible from Lisbon via Alcochete, just across the Vasco da Gama bridge. From here you can drive or walk into the leziria marshlands, one of Europe's most important staging sites for migrating water birds, including flamingo, black-tailed godwit and avocet.

Hilltop castle, Palmela

7 Óbidos

Óbidos is arguably the most picturesque town in Portugal. Contained within the walls of a 14th-century castle, it is filled with whitewashed houses with their edges painted ochre or blue, and their windows adorned with lace curtains and potted geraniums. The town was the wedding gift of Dom Dinis to his queen, Isabel of Aragon, in 1282.

8 Mafra

Mafra is home to an extravagant palace and monastery built for Dom João V, Portugal's 18th-century monarch, who had a weakness for excess of all kinds. The almost pyramidal proportions of its construction are entertainingly detailed in José Saramago's novel *Baltasar and Blimunda*. A section of Mafra's hunting grounds is now used for a wolf conservation project.

Palace interior at Mafra

9 Tomar

The UNESCO-listed Convento do Cristo is the main attraction of this Templar town in Central Portugal. Founded in 1160 by the Portuguese crusader Gualdim Pais, it follows the Manueline architecture style *(see p41)* with its plateresque façades and maritime motifs.

10 Ribatejo Wine Route

Some of the best wine producers in the Ribatejo region are clustered on the left bank of the Tejo, particularly between the towns of Almeirim and Alpiarça. Most welcome visitors. Seek out Quinta do Casal Branco, Quinta da Alorna, Fiuza & Bright and Quinta da Lagoalva de Cima.

TOP 10 BEAUTY SPOTS

Palace-pavilion at Monserrate

1 Monserrate
With a history of English gardeners and visitors, the stunning gardens and palace-pavilion of Monserrate remain popular *(see pp102–103)*.

2 Castelo dos Mouros
The steeply stepped walls of this attractive 8th-century castle offer some really fabulous views.

3 Penedo
This village on the high road from Sintra to the coast is misty and romantic in winter and a cool refuge in summer.

4 Peninha
This small sanctuary offers views of Europe's western edge, plus a small group of buildings with an intriguing history *(see p104)*.

5 Ursa
Stroll along this secluded beach out of season and take in the sheer beauty of the place *(see p45)*.

6 Guincho Coast
Cars drive very slowly – a rare thing in Portugal – along this beautifully scenic coast road *(see p101)*.

7 Portinho da Arrábida
One of the most protected beaches along the western seaboard looks as though it belongs in Croatia or Turkey.

8 Pancas and Around
If you prefer huge skies and endless views, head for this hamlet northeast of Alcochete, on the edge of the *lezíria*.

9 Cabo Espichel
The clifftop southwesternmost point of the Setúbal peninsula is in some ways more attractive than the better known Cabo da Roca.

10 Bucelas and Beyond
For a taste of inland Estremadura – and some superb white wine.

Lisbon Area by Area

Keep entrance, Castelo de São Jorge

Alfama, Castelo and the East

Cloister, Sé de Lisboa

Alfama's Arabic-sounding name recalls its past as an important district of Moorish Lisbon. No buildings survive from this era, but Alfama suffered little damage in the 1755 earthquake, so its medieval street plan has remained intact – and largely traffic-free. The Castelo neighbourhood at the top adjoins the higher hill district of Graça. To the south and east, Alfama descends to the river.

ALFAMA, CASTELO AND THE EAST

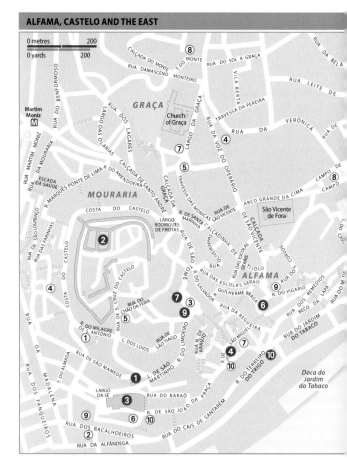

Museu do Teatro Romano

MAP N4 ▪ Rua São Mamede 3 ▪ 215 818 530 ▪ Open 10am–6pm Tue–Sun ▪ Adm ▪ www.museudelisboa.pt/pt/nucleos/teatro-romano

A Roman amphitheatre dating from the 1st century BC lies beneath the buildings just above the Sé de Lisboa. Not a lot has yet been excavated, but it seems to have been a sizable structure, seating up to 5,000. Excavations are ongoing, and visitors are offered an insight into the archaeological work that continues here, as well as at various other sites in central Lisbon.

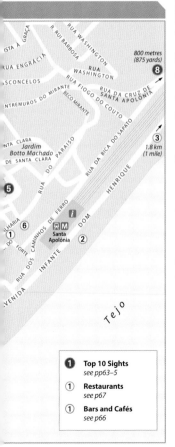

Castelo de São Jorge and Alfama

Castelo de São Jorge

The castle that crowns Alfama was the heart of the city in the Moorish era, and the site goes back to Phoenician times at least (see pp12–13). The picturesque residential area within the castle's outer walls is also called Castelo.

Sé de Lisboa

The English crusader Gilbert of Hastings, Lisbon's first bishop, oversaw the construction of the city's cathedral in the mid-12th century. The site was previously occupied by a mosque, parts of which have been excavated (see pp16–17).

Largo de São Miguel
MAP P4

You can reach this square in the heart of Alfama via steps from Largo das Portas do Sol; walk down next to Santa Luzia church and bear left after the first corner. This is the essence of Alfama: narrow alleys that older residents use as gardens, grills with sardines smoking, patios, archways and twisting stairs. The absence of cars lets children play everywhere. On 12 June every year, Largo de São Miguel is at the centre of the huge party thrown to honour St Anthony, Lisbon's most popular patron saint.

Top 10 Sights	see pp63–5
Restaurants	see p67
Bars and Cafés	see p66

⑤ Igreja de Santa Engrácia/Panteão Nacional

MAP R3 ■ Campo de Santa Clara ■ Open Apr–Sep:10am–6pm Tue–Sun (Oct–Mar: to 5pm) ■ Adm ■ www. panteaonacional.gov.pt

The soaring dome of Santa Engrácia is a landmark on Lisbon's low eastern skyline, but when you approach it on foot it seems to duck out of view at every turn. The dome was added in 1966 – 284 years after the construction of the church began. This in turn has enriched the Portuguese language with a saying that translates as "a job like Santa Engrácia", for any interminable project. The airy, marble-clad interior serves as the National Pantheon (see p40).

⑥ Santo Estevão
MAP Q4

The small esplanade in front of the Santo Estevão church is one of the area's best viewing points. Access is easy, if steep, from Largo do Chafariz de Dentro, at the foot of Alfama, where you will find one of the city's oldest public fountains (as well as the Fado Museum, so you can easily combine a visit to both). Just head up Rua dos Remédios and climb the Escadinhas de Santo Estevão steps on your left.

⑦ Largo das Portas do Sol
MAP P4

When the 28 tram gets to the top of the hill beyond the Sé de Lisboa, it squeezes between two buildings in what used to be the Moorish-era city walls. This spot gives one of the best

ST ANTHONY OF THE SARDINES

The celebration of St Anthony **(above)**, on 12 June, falls close to the feast days of other saints (São João and São Pedro, or John and Peter), resulting in a two-week party known as the *Festas dos Santos Populares*. In fact, the city has declared the whole month *Festas da Cidade*. But the real party is in Largo de São Miguel on 12 June, when tables are set up everywhere, grills are fired up and loaded with sardines, the wine and beer flow freely, and bands play.

views of Alfama and the river. Backtrack past the Santa Luzia church, and you reach the Miradouro de Santa Luzia, one of the city's official viewpoints (see p42). Across the street are two access routes to the castle. There are several outdoor cafés in the area.

⑧ Museu Nacional do Azulejo

Beyond Alfama, in the eastern Xabregas district, is the Tile Museum (see pp26–7), housed in a stunning former 16th-century convent with an elaborately decorated church.

View from Largo das Portas do Sol

Highlights include a small Manueline cloister, a 23-m (75-ft) panel of painted tiles showing Lisbon in the 1740s, and extensive collections of Moorish and Portuguese tiles. The café-restaurant is a pleasant place to take a break.

9 Fundação Ricardo do Espírito Santo Silva

MAP P4 ■ Largo das Portas do Sol 2 ■ 218 814 600 ■ Open 10am–5pm Wed–Mon ■ Adm

Named after the banker who bequeathed a 17th-century Alfama palace filled with his collections of decorative arts, this museum displays an extensive collection of Portuguese, French and English furniture in period settings. Next door are workshops for traditional crafts such as cabinet-making, gilding and bookbinding. The foundation also runs two schools of arts and crafts in other locations.

Display at the Museu do Fado

10 Museu do Fado

MAP Q4 ■ Largo do Chafariz do Dentro 1 ■ 218 823 470 ■ Open 10am–6pm Tue–Sun ■ Adm

Also called the Casa do Fado e da Guitarra Portuguesa, this museum is dedicated to Lisbon's most famous musical genre and to the mandolin-shaped Portuguese guitar. The instrument, whose strings are in pairs, combines with the singer's soaring tremolos to give *fado* – often compared with the blues – its unique sound. The museum is surprisingly modern, but its life-size replica of a *fado* venue – complete with singer, musicians, staff and customers – has an old-fashioned feel.

ALFAMA WANDERING

▶ MORNING

Alfama is really the sort of place to wander around if you want to explore old Lisbon. Like most labyrinthine medieval quarters it is quite small, but it seems large to the first-time visitor. Here are a few pointers, to help you on your way. The street that begins on the right side of the Sé de Lisboa, briefly called **Cruzes da Sé** and then **Rua de São João da Praça**, is a good point of entry. There are also some worthwhile cafés and bars here, including **Crafty Corner** *(see p66)*. Don't turn right off this street, or you'll be led down and out of the maze. Instead, keep going and follow it round. You'll eventually reach **Rua de São Pedro**, which leads down to **Largo do Chafariz de Dentro**, where there's a good choice of restaurants for lunch.

AFTERNOON

To return to the maze, head back up Rua de São Pedro and do a near 180-degree turn at the top to reach **Igreja de São Miguel**. Follow left turns by right turns and you should be able to weave your way to **Santo Estevão**. Should thirst overcome you, head down the steps to bar and restaurant **Pateo 13**. A brisk walk up Rua dos Remédios and then along Rua do Paraíso will get you to **Campo de Santa Clara** and, if it's Tuesday or Saturday, the **Feira da Ladra** flea market *(see p55)*. If it's not, stroll along to the Miradouro da Graça, the viewpoint near the **Esplanada da Igreja da Graça** *(see p66)*, and enjoy views of the castle *(see p12)*, downtown Lisbon and the 25 de Abril bridge.

See map on pp62–3

Bars and Cafés

Outdoor dining at Chapitô a Mesa

1 Chapitô a Mesa
MAP N4 ■ Costa do Castelo 7

This bar, café and restaurant offers a variety of seating and superb views.

2 Basílio
MAP N5 ■ Rua dos Bacalhoeiros 111

Enjoy breakfast or a mid-afternoon snack at this café in the old town. They offer pancakes, eggs and granola bowls, along with coffee and smoothies.

3 Portas do Sol
MAP P4 ■ Largo das Portas do Sol

This stylish café, bar and restaurant is right by the Portas do Sol viewpoint. The outdoor seating area affords views of the Tejo estuary and beyond.

4 Damas
MAP P2 ■ R. da Voz do Operário 60

Set in a former bakery, this inviting establishment is a bar, restaurant and concert hall, all rolled into one.

5 Botequim
MAP P2 ■ Largo da Graça 79

A daytime café, which transforms into a music- and poetry-reading venue by night. Enjoy the tapas and cocktails served in an alternative setting.

6 Duetos da Sé
MAP P5 ■ Travessa do Almargem 1b

Gastronomy meets art at this convivial café-bar situated right behind the cathedral. Enjoy soups, sandwiches and snacks, often with live music.

7 Esplanada da Igreja da Graça
MAP P2 ■ Largo da Graça

One of Lisbon's best café-table views is to be had from the esplanade by the vast Graça church (see p41). It is particularly attractive in the late afternoon on a sunny day.

8 Vino Vero
MAP H3 ■ Travessa do Monte 30

This well-stocked Italian wine bar landed in the Graça neighbourhood in 2019. It focuses on natural wines, which pair perfectly with the charcuterie and cheese boards. Come early for a seat on the terrace.

9 Outro Lado
MAP N5 ■ Beco do Arco Escuro 1

Situated right next to Lisbon's cathedral, this refreshing oasis offers different types of beer and has 15 craft beers on tap.

10 Crafty Corner
MAP P5 ■ Rua de São João da Praça 93–5

This rustic-style bar stands out with its arched ceilings and stone walls. There are 12 taps, all with Lisbon-based craft beer, plus snacks such as chicken wings. The empty kegs have been repurposed as seats surrounding large communal tables.

Restaurants

PRICE CATEGORIES

For a three-course meal for one with half
a bottle of wine (or equivalent meal),
taxes and extra charges.

€ under €20 ■ €€ €20–€40 ■ €€€ over €40

1 Taberna Sal Grosso
MAP R3 ■ Calçada do Forte 22
■ 910 137 713 ■ €€

Close to the National Pantheon, this
tavern serves delicious fresh fish.

2 Casanova
MAP R3 ■ Avenida Infante Dom
Henrique/Cais da Pedra, Armazém B,
Loja 7 ■ 218 877 532 ■ €€

Lisbon's best pizzas are served at this
lively restaurant with a terrace on the
quay. Arrive early to avoid waiting.

3 D'Avis
MAP C2 ■ Avenida Dom João II,
Parque das Nações ■ 218 681 354
■ Closed Sun ■ €€

Sample food from the Alentejo region
at this tavern. Try dishes of *porco
preto*, flavourful free-range Iberian pig.

4 O Velho Eurico
MAP G4 ■ Largo São
Cristóvão 3 ■ Closed Mon ■ €€

This no-frills restaurant serves a mix
of traditional Portuguese staples.
You can order a few dishes to share,
but the *arroz de pato* (duck rice) is
a must-try. Reservations by email
(reservas.ovelhoeurico@gmail.com).

5 Arco do Castelo
MAP N4 ■ Rua do Chão da Feira
25 ■ 218 876 598 ■ Closed Sun ■ €€

Genuine Goan restaurants like this
one are quite a rarity. Try specialities
like *sarapatel* (a spicy stew made
with meat, offal, blood and vinegar).

6 Faz Figura
MAP R3 ■ Rua do Paraíso 15b
■ 218 868 981 ■ Closed Mon & Sun D
■ €€€

Dig into delicious food and enjoy
the wonderful panoramic views

of the River Tagus from the
large terrace of this stylish
international restaurant.

7 Lautasco
MAP Q4 ■ Beco do Azinhal 7A
(off Rua de São Pedro) ■ 218 860 173
■ Closed Sun ■ €€

Traditional Portuguese fare is the
speciality of this informal restaurant,
decorated with rustic wooden panels.

8 Santa Clara dos Cogumelos
MAP Q2 ■ Campo de Santa Clara 7
■ 218 870 661 ■ Closed L Tue–Fri,
Sun & Mon ■ €€

There are splendid river views at
this unassuming restaurant that
specializes in mushroom dishes.

9 Do Vigário
MAP H4 ■ Rua do Vigário 74
■ 916 294 676 ■ Closed L Sun &
Mon ■ €

Crates with new and old records
sit alongside the tables at this cosy
restaurant. The menu lists a delicious selection of Portuguese tapas.

Live *fado* music at A Baíuca

10 A Baíuca
MAP H4 ■ Rua de São Miguel 20
■ 939 457 098 ■ Closed Tue, Wed, L ■ €€

Among other options, this tiny
restaurant serves up a delicious
bacalhau assado (roasted salt cod).
Amateur *fado* performances add
to the traditional ambience.

See map on pp62–3

🔟 Baixa to Restauradores

From the early 16th to mid-18th centuries, Lisbon's royal palace stood on the riverbank, around today's Praça do Comércio. It was the grand entrance to Lisbon, one of the world's great cities. Then in 1755 the earth shook, the ocean rose and fires raged – and the Paço Real and most of the medieval jumble of buildings behind it were gone. The Baixa we see was built on the ruins of lower Lisbon, to a different plan, in a different style, for a new era. Today this is the ageing heart of Lisbon, facing the challenges of depopulation, traffic, subsidence and modern shopping centres – but still going strong.

Carving at Igreja da Conceição Velha

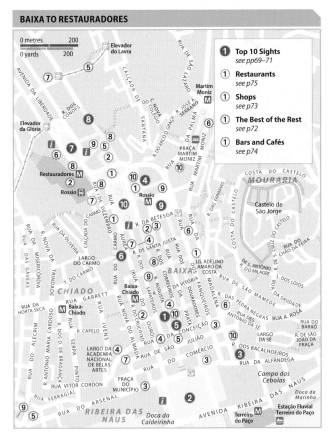

BAIXA TO RESTAURADORES

❶	**Top 10 Sights** see pp69–71
①	**Restaurants** see p75
①	**Shops** see p73
①	**The Best of the Rest** see p72
①	**Bars and Cafés** see p74

Shoppers on Rua Augusta

1 Rua Augusta
MAP M4–5

Lisbon's longest and grandest pedestrianized street runs through the middle of Baixa, from one corner of Rossio to a triumphal archway on Praça do Comércio. The arch, which commemorates the city's recovery after the 1755 earthquake, was added only in 1873. An allegorical figure of Glory stands atop it, crowning with wreaths the figures representing Genius and Bravery. Below, a gallery of national figureheads includes the Marquis of Pombal. The side of the arch facing Rua Augusta features a large clock, much consulted by the shoppers who throng the street.

2 Praça do Comércio
MAP M5

The broad riverfront square also known as Terreiro do Paço has regained some of its stature since cars were prohibited from parking there. It is surrounded on three sides by the elegant arcades of Pombal's reconstruction (see p37), and faces the river along the fourth. In the square is a statue of Dom José I, Portugal's ineffectual king at the time of the earthquake, who gazes at the river from his horseback perch, in a bronze by Machado de Castro. In the 15th century, the square was used as a slave port; you can uncover this dark side of its history on the African Lisbon tour (see p109).

3 Igreja da Conceição Velha
MAP N5 ■ Rua da Alfândega
■ Open 10am–1pm daily (3–8pm Mon–Fri & 3–6pm Sat)

This was the grand 16th-century Igreja da Misericórdia before the 1755 earthquake, which destroyed everything but the Manueline portal and one interior chapel. When it opened again in 1770, it was taken over by the congregation of another Baixa church that had been irreparably damaged in the quake, the Conceição Velha. The new church was very modest, and most visitors today come to admire the detailed portal. This features a carved image of Our Lady of Mercy, her long mantle held by two angels to shelter kneeling historical figures including Dom Manuel and Pope Leo. The Monument to the Enslaved People (see p70) will be erected nearby on Campo das Cebolas.

4 Igreja de São Domingos
MAP M3 ■ Largo de São Domingos ■ Open 7:30am–7pm daily

Dark and cavernous, the São Domingos church (see p40) is not much visited by tourists, despite its long history. As a result, it is a good place for quiet reflection.

Statue and arch, Praça do Comércio

⑤ Núcleo Arqueológico da Rua dos Correeiros

MAP M5 ▪ Rua dos Correeiros 21 ▪ 211 131 070 ▪ Closed Sun ▪ Guided tours in English and Portuguese: Hourly between 10am–5pm Mon–Sat (except 1pm) ▪ www.fundacaomillenniumbcp.pt/en/nucleo-arqueologico/

When a Portuguese bank began renovating its head office in the early 1990s, builders uncovered ancient remnants of Roman Lisbon. A small museum was set up. This revealed parts of what appears to have been a factory for making *garum* (fermented fish sauce). A section of mosaic floor uncovered in a separate structure suggests other, or later, uses.

The Santa Justa lift

⑥ Elevador de Santa Justa

MAP M4 ▪ Rua de Santa Justa ▪ Open 7:30am–11pm summer, 7:30am–9pm winter daily ▪ Adm for ride/views

You may be told that this iron lift was designed by Gustave Eiffel (of Paris tower fame), but in fact it is by Raoul Mesnier de Ponsard, his Portuguese pupil. There were once three such lifts in Lisbon's craggy cityscape, before the dawn of small delivery lorries. Today the Neo-Gothic lift (check out the exterior walls of the tower) whisks visitors from Baixa to the Carmo ruins (see p77). There are photo opportunities and a scenic terrace at the top.

MONUMENT TO THE ENSLAVED PEOPLE

More than two hundred years after the abolition of slavery in Portugal, Lisbon plans to unveil a Monument to the Enslaved People at Campo das Cebolas opposite Casa dos Bicos. The city council chose a design by Angolan artist Kiluanji Kia Henda called "Plantation – Prosperity and Nightmare" which depicts sugar cane plantations. Sugar cane was one of the goods traded in Brazil and Madeira during the Portuguese Age of Discovery. The metal plantation with 540 sugar canes in black lacquered aluminium will be a homage to enslaved people.

⑦ Praça dos Restauradores

MAP L2

This plaza and its monument were built when the old Passeio Público was turned into Avenida da Liberdade in the 1870s. It commemorates the restoration of the Portuguese monarchy in 1640. The obelisk is engraved with important dates from the restoration campaign, and is flanked by statues representing the Spirit of Independence and Victory. The surrounding square is dominated by traffic; shops, cafés, kiosks and restaurants cluster in its lower corners.

Obelisk, Praça dos Restauradores

8 Rua das Portas de Santo Antão
MAP L2

This long, partly pedestrianized street has food choices galore. The legendary Gambrinus restaurant sits next to the tiny A Ginjinha bar, and between these extremes is a clutch of seafood restaurants with outdoor seating, plus the atmospheric Casa do Alentejo, the cheerful Bonjardim, known for its piri-piri chicken (see p75).

Rua das Portas de Santo Antão

9 Praça da Figueira
MAP M3

After the earthquake, an open-air market was set up in what is now Praça da Figueira. It became the city's main vegetable market, and was eventually roofed with iron pavilions and cupolas. It joined next-door Rossio as Lisbon's bustling centre, scene of raucous Santo António celebrations in mid-June. Around special holidays such as Easter and Christmas, the square hosts the Mercado da Baixa, a food market offering mouthwatering treats ranging from freshly baked bread to local cheese.

10 Rossio
MAP L3–M3 ▪ Praça Dom Pedro IV

Rossio, officially Praça Dom Pedro IV, has been Lisbon's main square probably since Roman times. Surrounded by some of the city's grandest buildings before the earthquake, it was later outshone by the Praça do Comércio, but remains the city's cosmopolitan heart.

A STROLL THROUGH BAIXA

MORNING

Begin at the riverside gardens to the west of **Praça do Comércio** (see p69), where the old palace steps can still be seen. Cross the square and admire the views from the top of **Rua Augusta** (see p69). Turning right on Rua da Alfândega, take in the Manueline portal of **Igreja da Conceição Velha** (see p69). Then head up Rua da Madalena, and drop into the **Conserveira de Lisboa** (see p72) on the side street of Bacalhoeiros for a souvenir of tinned sardines. Turn left at Largo da Madalena and descend two blocks to the narrower Rua dos Douradoures, where you will find plenty of options for lunch.

AFTERNOON

Work your way through Baixa's grid, up to the main pedestrianized Rua Augusta. Look out for Rua de Santa Justa and a view of the Elevador de Santa Justa. Next stop is the top left corner of **Praça da Figueira**, for coffee and pastries at **Confeitaria Nacional** (see p74). Then walk up Rua Dom Antão de Almada, past fragrant shops selling herbs and other dried goods. On your right is one of Lisbon's oldest churches, **Igreja de São Domingos** (see p40). Slightly left and then straight ahead is **Rua das Portas de Santo Antão**. If you've already worked up an appetite, you couldn't be in a better area; for a pre-prandial drink, duck into the **A Ginjinha** bar (see p74) for a cherry liqueur.

See map on p68

The Best of the Rest

Interior of the Teatro Nacional Dona Maria II

① Teatro Nacional Dona Maria II

MAP L3 ▪ Praça Dom Pedro IV ▪ 213 250 800

The Neo-Classical building housing Portugal's national theatre was built around 1840, at the same time that Rossio was paved with its characteristic black and white cobblestones.

② Rossio Station

MAP L3 ▪ Between Rossio and Restauradores squares

Built in 1892, the old central station now serves Sintra *(see pp32–3)*. The statue on the façade is of Dom Sebastião, the boy king lost in battle in 1578.

③ Shops in Rua do Arsenal

MAP L5

A whiff of an older Lisbon lives on in shops selling dried fish, from *bacalhau* (salt cod) to octopus, dried goods, wine and some fresh produce.

④ Haberdashers in Rua da Conceição

MAP M5 ▪ Between Rua Augusta and Rua da Prata

Baixa shopkeepers may be buckling under competition from the shopping centres, but at this string of haberdashers' shops you can still buy a single button or length of lace.

⑤ Elevador do Lavra

MAP L1 ▪ Largo da Anunciada/Calçada do Lavra

The oldest Lisbon funicular, inaugurated in 1884, connects Restauradores with Campo de Santana, and travels to the Jardim do Torel viewpoint *(see 43)*.

⑥ Centro Comercial Mouraria

MAP N2 ▪ Praça Martim Moniz ▪ 218 880 904 ▪ Open 9am–8pm Mon–Sat

A six-level hotchpotch of small stores, mostly selling international foods, clothes and accessories.

⑦ Antiga Ervanária d'Anunciada

MAP L2 ▪ Largo da Anunciada 13–15 ▪ 213 427 997

Claiming to be Portugal's oldest herbalist, this shop sells vitamin super-cures as well as traditional dried herbs for infusions.

⑧ Monumento ao Calceteiro

MAP L3 ▪ Praça dos Restauradores

This statue pays homage to the *calceteiros*, the people who assemble the stones that make up Lisbon's famous black-and-white pavements. It features two bronze figures: a *calceteiro* shaping the stone and an assistant who is holding a giant hammer.

Plate from Arte Rústica

⑨ Arte Rústica

MAP M4 ▪ Rua Augusta 193 ▪ 213 461 004

This shop is stocked with regional crafts, hand-painted ceramics and embroidery.

⑩ Conserveira de Lisboa

MAP N5 ▪ Rua dos Bacalhoeiros 34 ▪ 218 864 009

Sardines and other tinned fish come in retro packages at this local store, open since the 1930s.

Shops

1 **Chapelaria Azevedo Rua**
MAP M3 ■ Praça Dom
Pedro IV 72 ■ 213 427 511

The famous hatter at the northeastern corner of Rossio has managed to stay in business for 120 years despite the vagaries of hat-wearing fashion.

2 **Manuel Tavares**
MAP M3 ■ Rua da Betesga 1
■ 213 424 209

A good, tourist-oriented deli between Rossio and Praça da Figueira, where samples of wine, cheese and ham are sometimes offered for tasting before purchase.

3 **Garrafeira Napoleão**
MAP N5 ■ Rua dos
Fanqueiros 70 ■ 218 861 108

This branch of the wine-shop chain offers a friendly, personalized service. There's a wide choice of table and fortified wines, as well as some spirits.

4 **Silva & Feijóo**
MAP M4 ■ Rua de São Nicolau
52 ■ 916 487 225

Visit this charming little souvenir chain shop to buy traditional handicrafts from Portugal. You can also find culinary treats such as canned fish and wine here.

5 **Retrosaria Bijou**
MAP M5 ■ Rua da Conceição
91 ■ 213 425 049

Trading since 1920, this delightful haberdashery brims with beautiful buttons, ribbons, trimmings, vivid fabrics and other fine wares, including knitting yarn and an assortment of needles and thimbles.

6 **Pollux**
MAP M4 ■ Rua da Madalena
251 ■ 218 811 200

Located round the back of the many-floored Pollux department store, this shop sells excellent Portuguese stainless-steel cookware, knives and other serious cooking aids.

7 **Discoteca Amália**
MAP M4 ■ Rua do Ouro 272
■ 213 420 939

Not a disco, but a "disc shop", which specializes in traditional Portuguese music. It is particularly renowned for its range of *fado* music, and for its merchandise commemorating famous *fado* singer Amália Rodrigues.

8 **Sapataria Lisbonense**
MAP M4 ■ Rua Augusta 202
■ 213 426 712

At this old-school shoe shop styles are good value and sport an inner label to remind you of Lisbon. It specializes in orthopaedic shoes.

Doll parts, Hospital de Bonecas

9 **Hospital de Bonecas**
MAP M3 ■ Praça da Figueira 7
■ 213 428 574

The doll's hospital is not much bigger than a doll's house, but full of perfectly healthy dolls, as well as clothes and furniture for them. Barbie is not much in evidence.

10 **Casa Pereira Da Conceição**
MAP M4 ■ Rua Augusta 102 ■ 916
487 834

Established in 1933, this delightful shop specializes in tea and coffee blends. It also offers delicious chocolates and traditional Portuguese sweets.

See map on p68

Bars and Cafés

1 Nicola
MAP L3 ■ Praça Dom Pedro IV 24

Rossio's premier outdoor café is well sited for people-watching. It has a venerable history and a handsome marble Art Deco interior. Downstairs is a restaurant. Coffee is cheaper at the bar and more expensive outside.

2 Penta Café
MAP M4 ■ Rua do Ouro 115 ■ Closed Sun

This café near Armazéns do Chiado attracts visitors with its supersized toasts, up to a metre long, and cakes. Perfect for a midday snack.

Confeitaria Nacional

3 Confeitaria Nacional
MAP M3 ■ Praça da Figueira 18

A Lisbon institution for its splendid cakes and pastries. It has a busy takeaway service and café tables inside under a mirrored ceiling.

4 Dear Breakfast
MAP G5 ■ Calçada de São Francisco 35

The bright interior of this popular brunch spot is dotted with marble tables. Head here for scrumptious pancakes and egg dishes.

5 The British Bar
MAP L6 ■ Rua Bernardino Costa 52

At what was once the Taverna Inglesa, haunt of Brits from local shipping firms, there is a wide selection of beers available here.

6 VIP Éden
MAP L2 ■ Praça dos Restauradores 24

Head-spinning views of downtown Lisbon are the main draw at this café at the top of the VIP Executive Suites Éden Aparthotel (see p117). Just ask at reception and press T for "terrace" in the elevator.

7 Trobadores
MAP G5 ■ Calçada de São Francisco 6A ■ Closed Sun & Mon

This medieval-style bar serves traditional Portuguese petiscos like flamed chorizo. Drinks are served in terracotta cups or giant horns. Make sure to try the *hidromel* (honey mead).

8 Beira Gare
MAP L3 ■ Around the corner at Praça Dom João da Câmara 4

Best known for its *bifanas* (spicy pork sandwiches), this popular place also serves a range of seafood dishes.

9 O'Gilin's
MAP K6 ■ Rua dos Remolares 8

Lisbon's first Irish pub is still the city's best. At weekends and on some weeknights there is live music.

10 A Ginjinha
MAP M3 ■ Largo de São Domingos 8

Ginjinha is Portuguese cherry liqueur and this tiny bar serves virtually nothing else, surviving for over 150 years on sheer single-mindedness.

The diminutive A Ginjinha

Restaurants

PRICE CATEGORIES

For a three-course meal for one with half a bottle of wine (or equivalent meal), taxes and extra charges.

€ under €20   €€ €20–€40   €€€ over €40

1 Oven Lisboa
MAP G4 ■ Rua dos Fanqueiros 232 ■ 218 273 826 ■ €€ ■ Closed Mon

Enjoy Indian and Nepalese cuisine in this upscale downtown restaurant, featuring a traditional tandoor oven.

2 Gambrinus
MAP L2 ■ Rua das Portas de Santo Antão 23 ■ 213 421 466 ■ €€€

This classic Lisbon address is as famous for its seafood dishes and "rich fish soup" as it is for its high prices and endless business lunches.

3 Martinho da Arcada
MAP M5 ■ Praça do Comércio 3 ■ 218 879 259 ■ €€

Once a favourite of literary figures such as Fernando Pessoa, this is a great setting in which to try some traditional Portuguese food.

4 A Licorista e o Bacalhoeiro
MAP M4 ■ Rua dos Sapateiros 222 ■ 213 431 415 ■ Closed Sun ■ €€

This cosy restaurant is named after the Portuguese trawlers that fished cod off the coast of Newfoundland.

5 A Provinciana
MAP L2 ■ Travessa do Forno 23–25 ■ 213 464 704 ■ Closed Sun ■ €

Try regional Portuguese cuisine including the *bacalhau à minhota* (fried codfish), a speciality at one of central Lisbon's best-value restaurants.

6 Prado
MAP G4 ■ Travessa Pedras Negras 2 ■ 210 534 649 ■ €€ ■ Closed L Tue & Wed; Sun & Mon

Sample a seasonal menu, paired with organic and natural wines, at this charming farm-to-table restaurant.

7 Leão d'Ouro
MAP L3 ■ Rua 1 de Dezembro 105 ■ 213 426 195 ■ €€

This cathedral-like restaurant is indeed a temple: to seafood. Specialities are oven-roasted octopus and cod.

Interior of Casa do Alentejo

8 Casa do Alentejo
MAP L2 ■ Rua das Portas de Santo Antão 58 (upstairs) ■ 213 405 140 ■ €€

This Neo-Moorish former palace is home to an association for people from the Alentejo region. The restaurant is open to all and serves simple Alentejan food in various memorable rooms.

9 Bonjardim Rei dos Frangos
MAP L2 ■ Travessa de Santo Antão 14 ■ 213 427 424 ■ €

Grilled chicken with *piri-piri* (chilli) is one of the fondest food memories many visitors take away from Portugal. This is one of the best places to sample it.

10 Varanda de Lisboa
MAP M3 ■ Hotel Mundial, Praça Martim Moniz 2 ■ 218 842 000 ■ €€

Diners can enjoy great views of the Baixa from this restaurant at the top of Hotel Mundial. The traditional Portuguese food is excellent and the service is exceptional.

See map on p68

🔟 Chiado and Bairro Alto

Chiado is where some of Lisbon's hill neighbourhoods, steeped in history, collided with the newer 18th-century layout of Baixa, Pombal's reconstructed city centre. Today, both areas are old and venerated, and packed with shops, but Chiado's history and cultural institutions give its commercial activities a gilt edge. Higher up is Bairro Alto – the "high neighbourhood" – a 16th-century maze of narrow streets framed by the wider lanes and longer blocks of later construction. It may be the district of Lisbon with the highest concentration of bars, but it is also a residential area and, at its western end, a quiet neighbourhood of grand old mansions.

Tile from Igreja de São Roque

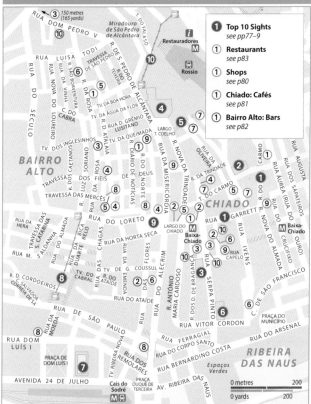

CHIADO AND BAIRRO ALTO

1 **Top 10 Sights**
see pp77–9

1 **Restaurants**
see p83

1 **Shops**
see p80

1 **Chiado: Cafés**
see p81

1 **Bairro Alto: Bars**
see p82

1 Rua do Carmo and Rua Garrett

MAP L4

Chiado's main arteries flow at right angles to each other, meeting in front of Armazéns do Chiado, a shopping centre housed in the shell of a burned-out department store. These partly pedestrianized and sometimes steeply inclined streets are among Lisbon's most bustling. Walk up from Baixa to the top, where the café A Brasileira *(see p81)* awaits.

Outdoor café tables, Rua Garrett

2 Largo and Igreja do Carmo

MAP L4 ■ Open 10am–7pm Mon–Sat (10am–6pm winter) ■ Adm

Accessible from Baixa either by walking or by using the Elevador de Santa Justa *(see p70)*, the ruins of the 14th-century Carmo church act as a memorial to the 1755 earthquake, which destroyed much of the structure *(see p41)*. The quiet square in front of the church seems an unlikely setting for one of the most dramatic events in modern Portuguese history. It was here that army tanks threatened the barracks of the National Guard, next to the Carmo church, where Marcelo Caetano, the country's dictator, had taken refuge on 25 April 1974. His surrender ended 42 years of fascist dictatorship in Portugal.

3 Teatro Nacional de São Carlos

MAP L5 ■ Rua Serpa Pinto 9 ■ 213 253 000 ■ Box office 1–7pm Mon–Fri ■ Ticket prices vary ■ www.tnsc.pt

Lisbon's opera house, dating from 1793, is regarded as the city's first Neo-Classical building. Its grand façade – the only side of the building decorated, in keeping with post-earthquake regulations – takes its cue from Milan's La Scala, although the floorplan resembles that of Naples' San Carlo opera. The grand interior owes more to the Baroque, with its gilt wood and marble. Outside, on the square the opera house sits on, is a statue dedicated to the writer Fernando Pessoa, who was born in one of the houses that line the square.

4 Igreja e Museu de São Roque

MAP K3 ■ Largo Trindade Coelho ■ Open 10am–6pm Tue–Sun

The Jesuit church of St Roch, built in the second half of the 16th century on the edge of what would become Bairro Alto, is a monument to the wealth of religious orders and the extravagance of Dom João V – although you wouldn't know it from the outside. Inside, its chapel to St John the Baptist has been described as one of the most expensive ever made. The church's museum of sacred art has an impressive collection of vestments and paintings *(see p41)*.

Chapel of St John the Baptist, Igreja de São Roque

Calçada do Duque

⑤ Calçada do Duque
MAP L3

This series of steps, from Largo Trindade Coelho to the bottom of Calçada do Carmo, is a treat. Along the gradual descent are Café Buenos Aires (see p83) and a number of other restaurants. The view of the Castelo de São Jorge, foreshortened above Rossio, is perfectly framed.

⑥ Museu Nacional de Arte Contemporânea do Chiado (MNAC)
MAP L5 ■ Rua Serpa Pinto 4 ■ Open 10am–1pm & 2–6pm Tue–Fri, 10am–2pm & 3–6pm Sat & Sun ■ Adm ■ www.museuartecontemporanea.gov.pt

Located near the Academy of Fine Arts, this is one of the best places to view Portuguese art from the mid-19th century on. The core collection focuses on the 1850–1950 period, but more recent acquisitions and temporary shows bring things up to date.

Elevador da Bica

LISBON'S BOHEMIAN DISTRICT

Bairro Alto's reputation for pleasure and mischief goes back several centuries. Even when this was a smart residential district in the 17th and 18th centuries, it had a shadier side. In the 19th century, after newspaper offices and printing shops moved in, the authorities decided to make Bairro Alto a zone of regulated prostitution. Today the area (below) is the heart of the city's nightlife, with *fado* houses and bars lining the streets.

⑦ Mercado da Ribeira
MAP K5 ■ Avenida 24 de Julho ■ 210 607 403 ■ Open Food hall: 10am–midnight Thu–Sun (to 1am Fri & Sat); Fish, fruit and vegetable market: 6am–2pm Mon–Sat

Lisbon's main fish, fruit and vegetable market is a riot of fresh produce. It also has a communal food hall, where a variety of stalls, bars and cafés offer cakes, cheeses and full meals.

⑧ Elevador da Bica
MAP K4 ■ Largo do Calhariz at Rua da Bica Duarte Belo ■ Open 7am–9pm Mon–Sat, 9am–9pm Sun & public holidays ■ €3.80 (funicular ticket for two rides)

Opened in 1892, this is the smallest of Lisbon's funiculars, passing through

the lively neighbourhood of Bica on its way between Largo do Calhariz and Rua de São Paulo. Like Lisbon's other funiculars, it is powered by an electric motor, which moves the cable to which both cars are attached so that they counterbalance each other and lighten the motor's load.

⑨ Praça Luís de Camões
MAP K4

This square, where Chiado meets Bairro Alto, is a favourite rendezvous point. It is named after the Portuguese poet laureate, whose heroic bronze, with other chroniclers and colleagues in stone around his feet, presides over the bright white stone oval traffic island. It used to be shaded by magnificent umbrella pines, but these have been replaced by still-puny poplars.

Praça Luís de Camões

⑩ Elevador da Glória
MAP K3 ▪ Praça dos Restauradores at Calçada da Glória ▪ Open 7:15am–11:55pm Mon–Fri, 8:45–11:55pm Sat, 9:15am–11:55pm Sun & public holidays ▪ €3.80 (funicular ticket for two rides)

Lisbon's best-known and now its busiest funicular links Restauradores with Bairro Alto. The second to be built, it was inaugurated in 1885. Formerly, the cars were open-top double-deckers, propelled by cog-rail and cable, with a water counterweight. Later on, steam power was used, but in 1915 the Glória went electric.

CHIADO TO BAIRRO ALTO AND THE BICA

▶ MORNING

Begin by the **Carmo** (see p77) ruins. If you're coming from Baixa, take the Elevador de Santa Justa or walk up. Crossing to the bottom left-hand corner of the square, take Travessa do Carmo, stopping for coffee at **Caffe di Marzano** (see p81) around the corner. Cross Largo Rafael Bordalo Pinheiro to Rua da Trindade and then Rua Nova da Trindade, on which turn right. Passing the famous Cervejaria Trindade on the right, you soon reach the top of **Calçada do Duque**. Straight ahead is **Igreja de São Roque** (see p77). Past the church, the street leads to the top of the **Elevador da Glória** and to the **Miradouro de São Pedro de Alcântara** (see p42), a garden with great views. For lunch, carry on up the street and try **Lost In** at no. 56d, or the steak house **La Paparrucha** at no.18/20.

AFTERNOON

After lunch, stroll along Bairro Alto, entering via Rua da Rosa on the other side of Rua Dom Pedro V. Keep track of Rua da Rosa, which will take you out of the area on the other side. Here, across the street, is the top of the **Elevador da Bica**. Ride it down to Rua de São Paulo and then head left towards Cais do Sodré, taking a drink at **O'Gilin's** or **The British Bar** (see p74). Otherwise, walk halfway up the steep hill again and turn left into one of the narrow streets to reach **Miradouro de Santa Catarina** (see p42) and afternoon refreshments in the open air.

See map on p76 ←

Shops

1 Luvaria Ulisses
MAP L4 ■ Rua do Carmo 87A
This small gem of a shop is the only one in Portugal selling just gloves. Hand sewn, they have a lifetime guarantee covering repairs.

2 Leitão & Irmão
MAP L4 ■ Largo do Chiado 16
Jewellery and silverware from a company that was appointed crown jewellers in 1875. Their pieces are held in museums and private collections the world over.

Leitão & Irmão "Viana Heart" pendant

3 Embaixada
MAP J2 ■ Praça do Príncipe Real 26
This trendy shopping centre, with 18 boutique-style establishments, sells a range of items, such as eco-friendly cosmetics, handcrafted jewellery and fine clothing. Open until 8pm on weekdays and 7pm on Sundays.

4 A Carioca
MAP L4 ■ Rua da Misericórdia 9
Coffee beans from Africa, Asia and South America are roasted on the premises and sold either freshly ground or whole at this specialist shop. Tea and hot chocolate are also available; try the chocolate sourced from São Tomé.

5 Vista Alegre
MAP L4 ■ Largo do Chiado 20–21
The work of Portugal's premier porcelain maker is wide-ranging: from modern to traditional designs, and from restrained tableware to exuberant decorative pieces.

6 A Vida Portuguesa
MAP L4 ■ Rua Anchieta 11
This attractive shop in the heart of the Chiado sells the best of Portuguese jewellery, ceramics and toys.

7 The Feeting Room
MAP G4 ■ Calçada do Sacramento 26 ■ www.thefeetingroom.com
Showcasing young local and independent designers, this concept store sells clothing, footwear and other accessories. There's also a small café inside serving speciality coffee.

8 El Dorado
MAP K4 ■ Rua do Norte 23
This retro fashion boutique stocks seriously collectable Victorian lace gowns, 1960s psychedelic tunics, motorbike jackets and other vintage apparel.

9 Armazéns do Chiado
MAP L4 ■ Rua do Carmo 2
In the restored shell of what was Lisbon's poshest department store (destroyed by fire in 1988) is the city's most central shopping centre. The larger retailers here include FNAC.

10 Livraria Bertrand
MAP L4 ■ Rua Garrett 73
The Bertrand chain has branches all over the city; this one is Lisbon's oldest bookshop, stocking a wide selection of English-language titles in its warren of rooms.

Coffee beans, A Carioca

Chiado: Cafés

A Brasileira
MAP L4 ▪ Rua Garrett 120

The city's most famous café is an Art Nouveau tunnel of florid stuccowork, mirrors and paintings from its 1920s heyday. The tables outside, where a bronze statue of poet Fernando Pessoa lingers today, are among Lisbon's most coveted.

Coffee at the counter, A Brasileira

② Bénard
MAP L4 ▪ Rua Garrett 104

"The other café" is, in fact, a tearoom serving cakes and pastries that some consider superior to those of its neighbour. Its outdoor tables serve as a welcome extension to A Brasileira's often crowded terrace.

③ Simpli Coffee Chiado
MAP F4 ▪ Largo de São Carlos 52 ▪ Closed Sun & Mon ▪ www.simpli.pt

This tranquil café overlooks the Teatro Nacional de São Carlos (p77). Fresco tables, freshly baked sweets and specialty coffee are all available.

④ Royale
MAP L4 ▪ Largo Rafael Bordalo Pinheiro 29

Light lunches, snacks and cakes are served in this elegant café, which has a small interior courtyard. The service is excellent.

⑤ Leitaria Académica
MAP L4 ▪ Largo do Carmo 1

This venerable milk bar is named after Lisbon's first university. Its outdoor tables in peaceful Largo do Carmo are popular. Hearty meals are also served.

⑥ Landeau
MAP F4 ▪ Rua das Flores 70 ▪ Closed Sun & Mon

Cosy café Landeau is famous for its delicious three-layered chocolate cake. Beyond the blue-and-white *azulejo* façade is a rustic interior with an exposed stone ceiling and wooden tables.

⑦ Caffe di Marzano
MAP L4 ▪ Largo Rafael Bordalo Pinheiro 32

Italy meets New York at this stylish corner café. The menu offers delicious paninis and cheese platters paired with classic cocktails, vermouths and coffee.

⑧ Café Janis
MAP K5 ▪ Rua da Moeda 1A

This trendy bistro is situated in the same square as Mercado da Ribeira (see p78). Open from breakfast to dinner, it serves a mix of French and Mediterranean dishes. The terrace is ideal for a late-night cocktail.

⑨ Kaffeehaus
MAP L5 ▪ Rua Anchieta 3

This busy café-bar brings a delightful dash of Vienna to the Portuguese capital. Grab an outside table in the sun and relax with a coffee and tasty apple strudel.

⑩ Café no Chiado
MAP L5 ▪ Largo do Picadeiro 10

A popular meeting place for writers, musicians and artists, this colourful café has shelves stacked with books and periodicals. It serves a range of delicious light meals and snacks. There is a beautiful outdoor terrace with wonderful views.

See map on p76

Bairro Alto: Bars

1 Artis
MAP K4 ■ Rua Diário de Notícias 95

Artis is one of Bairro Alto's most lived-in bars. It's a great place for those who like low lights, jazz and the buzz of conversation.

2 By the Wine
MAP K5 ■ Rua das Flores 41-43

Empty wine bottles decorate this bar's ceiling, but you can get a full one from the menu which features fortified wines like Moscatel. There are cheese and sausage boards to snack on, too.

3 Portas Largas
MAP K3 ■ Rua da Atalaia 105

This is the Bairro Alto in a nutshell. "Wide Doors", as it is called, is a rustic tavern-turned-bar, whose party spills out onto the street. The crowd is young, friendly and laid-back.

4 A Capela
MAP K4 ■ Rua da Atalaia 45

The decor of this DJ bar combines sparseness with extravagance. The deep yet narrow space can get extremely crowded – but always with an interesting mix of people.

5 Majong
MAP K4 ■ Rua da Atalaia 3

This is a long-established and a very popular watering hole that offers snacks and a good range of cocktails, including the gin-based *primo basílico*.

6 Loucos e Sonhadores
MAP F4 ■ Rua da Rosa 261

This alternative bar offers a more relaxed atmosphere than other Bairro Alto bars. The kitsch decor includes mismatched furniture, books and dismantled mannequins. Drinks are affordable and usually come with a free bowl of popcorn.

7 Toca da Raposa
MAP G4 ■ Rua da Condessa 45

Friendly bartenders mix bespoke cocktails in this cave-like bar just off Calçada do Duque. The dim lights and velvet seats feel miles away from Lisbon's traditional streets. Many of the base flavours are infused in-house.

8 Pensão Amor
MAP K5 ■ Rua do Alecrim 19

Eclectic music adds to the appeal of this Burlesque-themed bar.

9 Aché Cohiba
MAP K4 ■ Rua do Norte 121

Lisbon's liveliest Cuban bar promises a real taste of Havana, with frenzied DJ sessions and deadly cocktails.

10 Pavilhão Chinês
MAP K2 ■ Rua Dom Pedro V 89

One of the oldest bars in Bairro Alto, this place is something completely different. Every spare inch of wall space is covered with a bizarre collection of paintings, porcelain, Airfix models, dolls and hats.

Quirky interior of Pavilhão Chinês

Restaurants

PRICE CATEGORIES

For a three-course meal for one with half a bottle of wine (or equivalent meal), taxes and extra charges.

€ under €20 **€€** €20–€40 **€€€** over €40

1 Essencial

MAP F4 ■ Rua da Rosa 176 ■ 211 573 713 ■ Closed Sun & Mon ■ €€€

Local chef André Lança Cordeiro runs this intimate restaurant in the heart of Bairro Alto. Tasting menus are French-inspired.

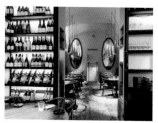

The elegant setting at Alma

2 Alma

MAP L4 ■ Rua Anchieta 15 ■ 213 470 650 ■ Closed Sun & Mon ■ €€€

A Michelin-starred restaurant, Alma offers a good choice of three-course à la carte and tasting menus, complemented by an impressive wine list.

3 Belcanto

MAP L4 ■ Rua Serpa Pinto 10A ■ 213 420 607 ■ Closed Sun, Mon ■ €€€

A long-established Chiado restaurant with two Michelin stars and a traditional ambience. The modern menu is sourced from local, seasonal produce.

4 Antigo 1 de Maio

MAP K4 ■ Rua da Atalaia 8 ■ 213 426 840 ■ Closed Sat L, Sun ■ €€

This family-run restaurant serves traditional Portuguese fare such as *carne do porco à alentejana* (pork with clams in garlic and olive oil).

5 Tapa Bucho

MAP K3 ■ Rua dos Mouros 19 ■ 914 566 392 ■ €€

Sample traditional Spanish tapas and Portuguese *petiscos* (small sharing plates) at this modern tavern near the Miradouro de São Pedro de Alcântara.

6 Tágide

MAP L5 ■ Largo da Academia Nacional de Belas Artes 18–20 ■ 213 404 010 ■ Closed Sun & Mon ■ €€€

This elegant restaurant serves delicious French-influenced Portuguese cuisine.

7 Café Buenos Aires

MAP L3 ■ Calçada Escadinhas do Duque 31B ■ 213 420 739 ■ €€

On the steps between Bairro Alto and Rossio, this cosy Argentinian-inspired place has tables outside and a menu that is not all meat.

8 Adega das Mercês

MAP K4 ■ Travessa das Mercês 2 ■ 213 424 492 ■ Closed Sun ■ €

Classic Bairro Alto restaurant specializing in grilled fish and meat. The portions are generous.

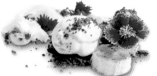

Dessert at Bistro 100 Maneiras

9 Bistro 100 Maneiras

MAP K3 ■ Largo da Trindade 9 ■ 910 307 575 ■ Closed Tue–Thu, Fri & Mon L ■ €€€

Try high-end dishes with a mix of east European and Portuguese flavours.

10 Casanostra

MAP K4 ■ Travessa do Poço da Cidade 60 ■ 213 425 931 ■ Closed Sat L ■ €€

One of Lisbon's first Italian restaurants remains one of its best, serving more than just good pasta.

See map on p76

🔟 Belém and the West

West Lisbon comprises a series of hills on either side of the Alcântara Valley, now filled with traffic rather than water. The city's former aqueduct spans the valley, disappearing into the Monsanto Park on Lisbon's highest hill. Opposite, the residential districts of Campo de Ourique, Estrela and Lapa descend in steep steps south towards the river. The waterfront from the Alcântara docks to Belém is straight and accessible, with the 25 de Abril bridge arching overhead.

Puppet in the Casa Fernando Pessoa

The expansive Jardim Botânico

1 Jardim Botânico
MAP J1–2 ■ Rua da Escola Politécnica 54 ■ 213 921 800 ■ Garden: 10am–8pm (until 5pm in winter) ■ Adm (free for under-10s)
Central Lisbon's sloping botanic garden was laid out in the second half of the 19th century, replacing Ajuda as the main showcase for flora, due

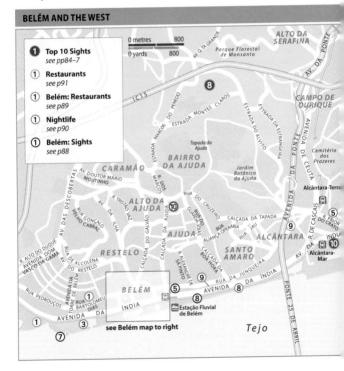

BELÉM AND THE WEST

1 Top 10 Sights
see pp84–7

1 Restaurants
see p91

1 Belém: Restaurants
see p89

1 Nightlife
see p90

1 Belém: Sights
see p88

to its more central location. The buildings at the top of the garden now house various museums, including the child-friendly Natural History and Science Museum *(see p49)*.

2 Casa Fernando Pessoa

MAP E4 ▪ Rua Coelho da Rocha 16–18 ▪ 213 913 270 ▪ Open 10am–6pm Tue–Sun ▪ Adm ▪ www.casafernando pessoa.pt

Portugal's great modernist poet Fernando Pessoa lived in this building from 1920 until his death in 1935. Later acquired and comprehensively redesigned by the city council, in 1993 it opened as a museum dedicated to Pessoa and to poetry. It houses the poet's personal library, books about him, and a collection of Portuguese and foreign poetry. There is also a space for temporary exhibitions and events, some of Pessoa's furniture, and the poet's room, which is

"recreated" at irregular intervals by invited artists. There's a restaurant in the small, modernist-style back garden.

Pastéis de Belém

3 Belém

Lisbon's westernmost district retains pleasant contrasts with the city centre. Refreshing river breezes and a cluster of some of Lisbon's main sights *(see p88)* contribute to Belém's appeal, along with the famed bakery Pastéis de Belém – the original creator of Lisbon's famous *pastel de nata*.

4 Estrela

MAP E4 ▪ Praça da Estrela

The area between Campo de Ourique and Lapa takes its name from the Basílica da Estrela *(see p40)*, opposite the entrance to central Lisbon's most agreeable park, Jardim da Estrela. It is a distinctly British part of Lisbon, with the British embassy and English Cemetery (where Henry Fielding is buried) close by.

5 Assembleia da República

MAP F4 ▪ Rua de São Bento ▪ 213 910 843 ▪ Guided tours available

This impressive building has been the seat of the Portuguese parliament since 1833, when the Benedictine monks of the Convento de São Bento da Saúde were evicted – a year before the dissolution of religious orders. The vast monastery was adapted in fits and starts; today's formal Neo-Classical building was designed at the end of the 19th century.

6 Museu da Marioneta

MAP F5 ▪ Rua da Esperança 146 (Convento das Bernardas) ▪ 213 942 810 ▪ Open 10am–6pm Tue–Sun ▪ Adm

Lisbon's Puppet Museum has a collection of over 400 puppets from all over the world, as well as scenery, props and machinery for puppet shows. It is housed in a former convent, which it shares with housing and the gourmet restaurant A Travessa (see p52). The museum also puts on shows and has puppetmaking workshops for school groups.

Mask from the Museu da Marioneta

7 Museu Nacional de Arte Antiga

Portugal's national museum (see pp18–19) holds some of the country's greatest artistic treasures, as well as foreign masterpieces such as Bosch's *The Temptations of St Anthony* – a painting about the Egyptian St Anthony, founder of Christian monasticism, rather than St Anthony of Padua, Lisbon's most popular patron saint.

Detail, *The Temptations of St Anthony*

A GOLDEN GATE FOR EUROPE

By the time the steel suspension bridge (above) was built across the Tejo in 1962–6, bridges had been proposed at various sites for nearly a century. Similar in design to San Francisco's Golden Gate bridge, Ponte Salazar (as it was originally called) is just over 1 km (about half a mile) long, which made it Europe's longest bridge when it opened in 1966. Its two towers are just under 200 m (650 ft) tall. Renamed Ponte 25 de Abril for the date of the Carnation Revolution in 1974, it has been adapted to increasing traffic over the years by squeezing in extra lanes and adding a railway crossing underneath. The 1998 opening of the Vasco da Gama bridge has relieved the bridge's notorious traffic jams.

8 Monsanto

MAP D2

Leafy and green, Monsanto is Lisbon's largest wooded area and its highest hill. It is the best place to go around central Lisbon for the smell of pine trees, a fresh breeze, and a walk with soil underfoot. Fitness equipment has been installed and paths have been laid out for walking, as well as cycling. There are a number of fenced-off recreational areas, including children's parks (see p48), tennis courts, a shooting range, a campsite and a rugby pitch. It's an area well worth exploring.

9 Aqueduto das Águas Livres

MAP F3 ▪ 218 100 215 ▪ Open 10am–5:30pm Tue–Sun ▪ Adm

Lisbon's long-legged aqueduct was commissioned by Dom João V in the early 18th century, and aimed to increase the city's supply of drinking water by drawing in fresh water from springs at the nearby parish of Caneças. Funded by a sales tax on products such as olive oil, meat and wine, construction on the aqueduct started in 1731, and by 1748 it was beginning to bring water into the city. Officially completed in 1799, the aqueduct carried water across 58 km (36 miles) of ducting. The system was only taken out of service in 1967. The Museu da Água organizes walks across the aqueduct.

The 18th-century arches of the Aqueduto das Águas Livres

⑩ Museu do Oriente

MAP D5 ■ Avenida Brasília, Doca de Alcântara (Norte) ■ 213 585 200 ■ Open 10am–6pm Tue–Sun (8pm Fri) ■ Adm (free 6–8pm Fri)

Located in an old dockside building, this fascinating museum celebrates Portugal's links with Asia across the ages. Highlights include a magnificent collection of 17th- and 18th-century Chinese and Japanese folding screens, as well as rare pieces of Ming porcelain and Namban art. Perhaps the most popular attraction is the Kwok On Collection, which consists of costumes, musical instruments, puppets and etchings from Japan, Korea, Myanmar (Burma), Cambodia and Iran.

A WALK THROUGH WEST LISBON

▶ MORNING

Begin by catching the 28 tram to its terminus at **Prazeres** *(see p46)*. Visit the cemetery of the same name, then stroll along Rua Saraiva de Carvalho past the large **Santo Condestável** church, with its attractive stained-glass windows. Drop into **Campo de Ourique** market *(see p54)* and pick up some fresh fruit, or just whet your appetite for lunch. Then head right along Rua Coelho da Rocha and visit **Casa Fernando Pessoa** *(see p85)*. Lunch here, or at the cosy **Tasca da Esquina** *(see p91)*, in Rua Domingos Sequeira.

AFTERNOON

After lunch, walk all the way down Rua Coelho da Rocha, turn right into Rua da Estrela, and proceed downhill to one of the corner entrances of **Jardim da Estrela** *(see p57)*, where you can absorb the peace of the park. When you're ready, head for the main entrance and you'll see the **Basílica da Estrela** *(see p40)* across the square. After a visit, make your way through Lapa via Rua João de Deus, which enters it on the left of the basilica. Follow the tram tracks round and then down Rua de São Domingos – veer off to left or right for extended Lapa views. Return to Rua de São Domingos and continue until you reach steps leading down to Rua das Janelas Verdes and the **Museu Nacional de Arte Antiga (MNAA)** *(see pp18–19)*.

See map on pp84–5 ←

Belém: Sights

Padrão dos Descobrimentos

1 Padrão dos Descobrimentos

MAP B6 ■ Avenida de Brasília ■ Open Mar–Sep: 10am–7pm daily (Oct–Feb: to 6pm) ■ Adm ■ www.padraodos descobrimentos.pt

Created in 1960 on the 500th anniversary of Henry the Navigator's death (see p37), this monument takes the form of the prow of a ship.

2 Palácio de Belém

MAP B6 ■ Praça Afonso de Albuquerque ■ 213 614 660 ■ Museum: Open 10am–6pm Tue–Fri, 10am–1pm & 2–6pm Sat & Sun (Palace and gardens closed to public) ■ Adm (free 10am–1pm Sun)

This 16th-century palace, altered by Dom João V, is the working residence of Portugal's president. It houses the Museu da Presidência da República.

3 Mosteiro dos Jerónimos

Portugal's greatest national monument is emblematic of the country's Manueline style. Dom Manuel I built the monastery and abbey in thanks for Portugal's maritime voyages (see pp14–15).

4 Museu de Arqueologia

MAP A6 ■ Praça do Império ■ 213 620 000 ■ Closed for renovation until 2025 ■ Adm

This museum exhibits archaeological finds from the Iron Age onwards.

5 Museu Nacional dos Coches

MAP B6 ■ Avenida da Índia 136 ■ 210 732 319 ■ Open 10am–6pm Tue–Sun ■ Adm ■ www.museu-doscoches.gov.pt/pt

This fascinating museum showcases historic coaches, including one made for Pope Clement XI.

6 Museu Coleção Berardo

MAP A6 ■ Praça do Império, Belém ■ Adm (free Sat) ■ www. museuberardo.pt

This collection of modern art includes works by Picasso and Andy Warhol.

7 Torre de Belém

For many, this defensive tower is the masterpiece of the Manueline style (see pp22–3).

8 MAAT (Museum of Art, Architecture and Technology)

MAP B6 ■ Avenida de Brasília ■ Open 10am–7pm Wed–Mon ■ Adm (free first Sun) ■ www.maat.pt

This modern art museum stands out with its striking wavy structure. Exhibits here focus on the connection between art and technology.

9 Jardim Botânico Tropical

MAP B5–6 ■ Largo dos Jerónimos ■ 213 921 808 ■ Open 10am–8pm daily (to 5pm winter) ■ Adm

This garden of tropical trees and plants – the research centre of the Institute for Tropical Sciences – is an oasis in the tourist bustle of Belém.

10 Palácio da Ajuda

MAP B5 ■ Largo da Ajuda ■ 213 620 264 ■ Open 10am–6pm Fri–Wed ■ Adm

The Neo-Classical Ajuda palace was left unfinished in 1807 when the royal family was forced into exile in Brazil.

Belém: Restaurants

1 Nunes
MAP A6 ■ Rua Bartolomeu Dias 172 ■ 213 019 899 ■ Closed Mon ■ €€ ■ www.nunesmarisqueira.pt

Located close to Lisbon's top tourist attractions, Nunes is renowned for its fresh seafood.

2 Solar do Embaixador
MAP B6 ■ Rua do Embaixador 210 ■ 213 625 111 ■ €

Tasty Brazilian specialities share the menu with more traditional Portuguese fare at this jolly restaurant in a Belém backstreet.

3 Vela Latina
MAP A6 ■ Doca do Bom Sucesso ■ 213 017 118 ■ Closed Sun D ■ €€

Overlooking the Bom Sucesso dock, this place specializes in creative fish and seafood dishes. Try the *filetes de pescada* (hake fillets).

4 Nosolo Itália
MAP B6 ■ Avenida de Brasília 202 ■ 213 015 969 ■ €€

Fine river views and a wide choice (for vegetarians, too) of pastas, pizzas and salads are on offer here.

5 Pão Pão Queijo Queijo
MAP A6 ■ Rua de Belém 126 ■ 213 626 369 ■ €

Facing the Mosteiro dos Jerónimos, this affordable restaurant has been serving stuffed baguettes and pita bread to passersby since 1996.

6 Belém 2 a 8
MAP B6 ■ Rua de Belém 2 ■ 213 639 055 ■ €€

Enjoy Portuguese cuisine at this brightly decorated place next to the president's palace.

7 Este Oeste
MAP A6 ■ Centro Cultural de Belém, Praça do Império ■ 914 914 505 ■ €€

An open-plan restaurant with magnificent river views, Este Oeste specializes in Italian and Japanese cuisine, with dishes such as wood-baked pizza and freshly made sushi.

8 Café In
MAP C6 ■ Avenida de Brasília, Pavilhão Nascente 311 ■ 213 626 248 ■ €€

With a popular terrace, a groovy retro bar and a slightly more formal restaurant, this low building on the riverside is busy all day. Grilled fish and seafood dominate the menu.

9 Alecrim no Prato
MAP C6 ■ Rua da Junqueira 207 ■ 213 621 804 ■ Closed Sun & Mon D ■ €€

Close to the MAAT museum, this friendly restaurant serves a range of Italian and Portuguese dishes, such as steaks and seafood risottos. There's also a good wine selection.

Outdoor seating at Alecrim no Prato

10 Taberna dos Ferreiros
MAP A6 ■ Travessa Ferreiros a Belém 5 ■ 215 873 837 ■ Closed Mon & Sun D ■ €€

Tucked away in a small alley, this cosy restaurant offers a modern take on traditional Portuguese food. Highlights include codfish and tuna.

See map on pp84–5

Nightlife

Laid-back club and venue Bar Lounge

1 Bar Lounge
MAP J5 ■ **Rua da Moeda 1**

This friendly and relaxed venue plays alternative music with regular live music sessions (see p50).

2 Trumps
MAP F4 ■ **Rua da Imprensa Nacional 104B**

A mainstay of Lisbon's LGBTQ+ scene, this mixed club, spread over two levels, has several bar areas and a dance floor.

3 Finalmente
MAP F4 ■ **Rua da Palmeira 38**

Another popular spot on the Lisbon LGBTQ+ scene, Finalmente has a small dance floor and regular drag shows. The party tends to kick off late, but it can get very lively as the night draws on.

4 Foxtrot
MAP F4 ■ **Travessa de Santa Teresa 28**

With a rambling series of rooms, a courtyard, pool tables and kitschy decor, this old-style bar has become a quintessential Lisbon hang-out.

5 Quimera Brewpub
MAP D5 ■ **Rua Prior do Crato 6**
■ **Closed Mon & Tue**

An 18th-century royal tunnel turned into a craft beer pub in Alcântara.

6 Titanic Sur Mer
MAP F5 ■ **Cais do Gás**

This riverfront club offers weekly live gigs and cabaret shows. There are free jazz concerts on Mondays.

7 Jamaica
MAP F5
■ **Cais do Gás**
■ **Closed Sun & Mon**

After 50 years of drawing the crowds to Pink Street (p51), Jamaica moved to Cais do Gás in 2022. The new space is nearly double in size, with room for 300 people. Rock and pop classics remain part of the standard playlist.

8 Friends Bairro Alto
MAP K3 ■ **Travessa da Água da Flor 17**

Set in the bustling district of Bairro Alto, this LGBTQ+ bar serves tapas and cocktails and often hosts pop music parties.

9 O Bar Mais Triste da Cidade
MAP E5 ■ **Calçada Ribeiro Santos 25**
■ **Closed Sun**

"The saddest bar in the city" serves fine whiskey paired with melancholic piano acts. The decor is anything but sad, though, with shimmery fringed curtains backing the counter.

10 B.Leza
MAP J6 ■ **Cais da Ribeira Nova, Armazém B** ■ **Wed–Sun**

With a wonderful riverside setting, this is Lisbon's top venue for live African and other world music performances. The club first appeared in mid-1990s, and offers live music, hosts regular dance workshops and guest DJ sessions.

Restaurants

1 Darwin's Café
MAP B3 ■ Avenida Brasília ■ 210 480 222 ■ €€

This waterfront restaurant near Torre de Belém serves delicious pasta and risotto dishes in a stylish environment.

2 Kais/Adega do Kais
MAP E5 ■ Rua do Cintura do Porto de Lisboa, Cais da Viscondessa ■ 213 932 930 ■ Closed L; Sun & Mon ■ €€€

Housed in a former engine shed, Kais offers a modern Portuguese menu. Adega do Kais, in the basement, is a traditional *rodízio* (rotisserie), serving a range of dishes for a fixed price.

3 Último Porto
MAP E5 ■ Rua General Gomes Araújo 1, Rocha do Conde de Óbidos ■ 213 979 498 ■ Closed D and Sun ■ €€

This restaurant is hidden between shipping containers near the Alcântara docks. Grilled seafood is the speciality here, with favourites including grouper and cuttlefish.

4 Senhor Uva
MAP E4 ■ Rua de Santo Amaro 66A ■ 213 960 917 ■ Closed L ■ €€

Translated as "Mr Grape", this cosy restaurant serves high-end vegetarian dishes paired with local organic wines.

5 Clube de Jornalistas
MAP E4 ■ Rua das Trinas 129 ■ 213 977 138 ■ €€

This attractive restaurant with an inner courtyard serves top-notch contemporary international food.

6 Arkhe
MAP F5 ■ Boqueirão do Duro 46 ■ 211 395 258 ■ Closed Mon L; Sat & Sun ■ €€

This lovely vegetarian restaurant serves delicious vegetable and meat-substitute dishes.

7 Tasca da Esquina
MAP E4 ■ Rua Domingos Sequeira 41c ■ 210 993 939 ■ Closed Tue & Wed ■ €€

Enjoy fried hake or tuna with sweet potato at this modern Lapa restaurant.

Pretty setting at Tasca da Esquina

8 A Travessa
MAP F5 ■ Travessa do Convento das Bernardas 12 ■ 213 902 034 ■ Closed Sun, L Mon–Sat ■ €€€

This is one of Lisbon's most characterful restaurants in terms of both location and food (see p52).

9 O Mercado
MAP D5 ■ Rua Leão de Oliveira 19 ■ 213 649 113 ■ Closed Sun D and Mon ■ €€

Set in a market building, this restaurant serves fresh local dishes.

10 Noobai Café
MAP J5 ■ Miradouro de Santa Catarina ■ 213 465 014 ■ €

Enjoy river views while snacking on wholesome soups, healthy salads and light tapas.

See map on pp84–5

🔟 Avenida and North Lisbon

Avenida da Liberdade extends northwards from Restauradores at a slight incline. It ends at the roundabout named after the Marquis of Pombal, who became Lisbon's *de facto* head of government after the 1755 earthquake. His statue stands at the centre of the swirl of traffic, flanked by a lion, surveying the city centre he created. If you continue up to the top of Parque Eduardo VII and look to your right, Lisbon's early 20th-century northern extensions stretch out before you. Closer at hand is the esteemed Gulbenkian museum; further afield, the 21st-century vistas of Parque das Nações.

Fan, Casa-Museu Fundação Medeiros e Almeida

① Museu Calouste Gulbenkian

Founded on the private collections and fortune of Armenian exile Calouste Gulbenkian, this museum *(see pp30–31)* is one of Lisbon's most satisfying sights. Inaugurated in 1969, it was purpose-built to display the wealthy oil magnate's bequest to the nation. It contains one of the most impressive collections of fine and decorative art in Europe.

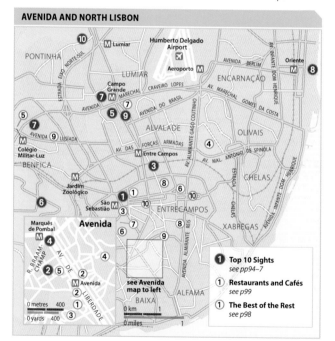

AVENIDA AND NORTH LISBON

Top 10 Sights
see pp94–7

Restaurants and Cafés
see p99

The Best of the Rest
see p98

Previous pages *Palácio Nacional da Pena, Sintra*

A Drawing Room in Casa-Museu Fundação Medeiros e Almeida

② Casa-Museu Fundação Medeiros e Almeida

MAP F3 ▪ Rua Rosa Araújo 41 ▪ 213 547 892 ▪ Open 10am–5pm Mon–Sat ▪ Adm (free first Sat 10am–1pm) ▪ www.museumedeirosealmeida.pt.

This treasure trove of a museum was the home of businessman and private collector António Medeiros e Almeida, who died in 1986. His collection of some 2,000 objects is astonishing: there are 25 rooms featuring French and Flemish tapestries, English silver, ornate furniture, priceless paintings and Chinese porcelain. Some of the most valuable items include bronze wall fountains from the Palace of Versailles, a silver dinner service that once belonged to Napoleon and a 17th-century clock made for Queen Catherine of Bragança.

③ Campo Pequeno

MAP F1 ▪ 217 998 450 ▪ Adm for events varies ▪ www. campopequeno.com

One of Lisbon's most striking buildings, this red-brick Neo-Moorish bullring from 1892 has onion cupolas and keyhole windows. It stands on a spot where bullfights *(see p96)* have been held since the first half of the 18th century. Many concerts and trade shows take place here. Following restoration, a shopping complex was constructed underneath the building; it contains shops, a food court and a cinema with eight screening rooms.

④ Marquês de Pombal Rotunda and Parque Eduardo VII

MAP F2–3

The roundabout where Pombal and his lion pose was the northern limit of the city he conceived. The orderly park behind him was first laid out in the late 19th century as a green extension of Avenida da Liberdade, replacing the pedestrian Passeio Público that the Avenida had usurped. In 1903, Parque da Liberdade was renamed in honour of the visiting English King Edward VII. It is really more of a steeply sloping promenade than a park. For proper greenery, seek out the Estufa Fria and Estufa Quente greenhouses along the park's northwestern edge. A walk to the top is rewarded with good views, the Linha d'Água café and Eleven restaurant *(see p53)*.

Parque Eduardo VII and the Marquês de Pombal Rotunda

5 Museu de Lisboa

MAP C1 ■ Campo Grande 245
■ 217 513 200 ■ Open 10am–6pm
Tue–Sun ■ Adm ■ www.museude
lisboa.pt/pt/nucleos/palacio-pimenta

The museum is housed in the 18th-century Palácio Pimenta, at the top of Campo Grande. The palace itself is worth seeing, particularly for the unusual kitchen tiles depicting animal carcasses hung to tenderize. The permanent exhibition traces Lisbon's development from the earliest settlements along the Tejo. Perhaps the most evocative display is the large 3-D model of Lisbon as it is believed to have looked before the earthquake in 1755.

Tile in the Museu de Lisboa

6 Palácio dos Marqueses da Fronteira

MAP B2 ■ Largo de São Domingos de Benfica 1 ■ Guided palace tours Mon–Sat; Jun–Sep: 10:30am, 11am, 11:30am, noon; Oct–May: 11am, noon; Gardens: 10am–5pm Mon–Fri (to 1pm Sat) ■ Adm ■ https://fronteira-alorna.pt

A 17th-century former hunting pavilion, expanded after the 1755 earthquake, this manor house and its gardens are really rewarding sights. The formal gardens are full of statues and tiled panels, from busts of Portuguese kings to allegorical representations of the seasons and the zodiac. Highlights inside the palace include the Battle Room, featuring depictions of battles during the War of Restoration against Spain – in which the first Marquis da Fronteira fought. Fronteira Palace is still owned and lived in by the current Marquis, who collects contemporary art and sometimes stages exhibitions.

Tilework, Palácio dos Marqueses da Fronteira

7 Football Stadiums

MAP B1 & B2 ■ Benfica: Av. Eusébio da Silva Ferreira; 707 200 100 ■ Sporting: Rua Professor Fernando da Fonseca; 217 516 000 ■ Match tickets from €20

Lisbon's two main football teams, Benfica and Sporting, both rebuilt their stadiums for the Euro 2004 championships, held in Portugal. Sporting's green-and-yellow Estádio José Alvalade is on the northern city limits. A short distance west is Benfica's red Estádio da Luz. Both teams have interesting museums and offer guided tours of the stadiums.

Parque das Nações waterfront

8 Parque das Nações

The former Expo 98 site is now a business and leisure area, with a variety of sights (see pp20–21).

9 Jardim Mário Soares

MAP C2 ■ Campo Grande ■ Open 24 hours daily; facilities inside (padel club, gym and kiosks) opens around 10am ■ Adm

This garden has cafés, a children's playground and sports facilities. Rent a boat or enjoy a stroll through this green oasis (see p37).

10 Parque do Monteiro-Mor

MAP B1 ■ Largo Júlio de Castilho ■ 217 567 620 ■ Park & Costume museum: Open 10am–1pm & 2–6pm Tue–Sun; Theatre museum: 10am–1pm & 2–6pm Tue–Sun ■ Adm

Despite its unpromising location, this lovely Italianate park is one of the city's best oases. With its palace – now housing two interesting museums devoted to Theatre and Costume – it is a reminder of what Lisbon's hinterland was once like.

TO THE GULBENKIAN AND BEYOND

▶ **MORNING**

Begin at the **Pombal Roundabout**, where you can study its various representations of tidal waves, destruction, and the enlightened despot's many reforms. Cross back to the bottom of **Parque Eduardo VII** (see p43) and set out for the summit; be aware that the walk is unshaded and it gets very hot in summer. If you need a break, dive into the cool of the **Estufa Fria** (see p98) and **Quente greenhouses** (see p95) . At the top, ponder the symbolism of João Cutileiro's **Monument to 25 April** and its contrast with Keil do Amaral's **twin columns**. Then climb the last bit of the hill to **Linha d'Água**; have lunch here, or enjoy a gourmet meal at the adjacent **Eleven** (see p99).

AFTERNOON

After lunch, continue past **El Corte Inglés** (see p98) and on to the side entrance of the **Museu Calouste Gulbenkian** (see pp30–31), at the north end of Avenida António Augusto de Aguiar. Expect to spend most of the afternoon in the museum – or give it a quick browse and come back later. Stroll through the park and exit on Rua Marquês de Sá Bandeira, then take Avenida Miguel Bombarda for a taste of the **Avenidas Novas**. Turn left onto Avenida da República and walk a few blocks north to admire **Campo Pequeno's** (see p95) impressive Neo-Moorish building. Stop in for a drink in the surrounding park before a spot of window-shopping.

See map on p94

The Best of the Rest

1 Hot Clube
MAP K1 ■ Praça da Alegria 48

Lisbon's oldest jazz club is indifferent to shifting fashions. Inside this small basement club, the gap between artists and audience evaporates.

2 Avenida Designer Shops
MAP F3 ■ Avenida da Liberdade

The former Passeio Público (Public Promenade) still hasn't recovered from the introduction of vehicles over a century ago. However, the appearance of international designer shops shows that Lisbon's main avenue has regained some of its pedigree.

3 El Corte Inglés
MAP F2 ■ Avenida António Augusto de Aguiar

The Spanish chain has one of its largest complexes in Lisbon. It includes the city's only true department store, plus restaurants, cinemas and luxury apartments.

4 Parque da Bela Vista
Avenida Gago Coutinho

A large urban park, Bela Vista hosts the Rock in Rio festival, which takes place in even-numbered years.

5 Centro Colombo
MAP B2 ■ Avenida Lusíada ■ Open 10am–midnight daily

Described as the biggest shopping centre in the Iberian peninsula, Colombo has more than 340 shops, plus restaurants and cinemas.

Centro Colombo

6 Estufa Fria
MAP F2 ■ Parque Eduardo VII

One of the most beautiful botanical attractions in Lisbon, the "Cold Greenhouse" has hundreds of plant specimens from all over the world, and sparkling waterfalls and brooks.

Cartoon in the Museu Rafael Bordalo Pinheiro

7 Museu Rafael Bordalo Pinheiro
MAP C1 ■ Campo Grande 382 ■ 215 818 540 ■ Open 10am–6pm Tue–Sun ■ Adm

This museum, dedicated to Portugal's best-known caricaturist and ceramic artist, offers a thorough but light-hearted look at Portugal's history.

8 Culturgest
MAP G1 ■ Rua Arco do Cego ■ 217 905 155 ■ Open 11am–6pm Tue–Sun ■ Adm

Housed in the Post-Modern headquarters of a state-owned bank, Culturgest stages music, dance, theatre and exhibitions.

9 Benfica
MAP B2 ■ Estrada de Benfica

This suburb, now a part of the city, has its own rhythm. The football team did not start here – it moved in – but this is still one of Lisbon's proudest *bairros*.

10 Alameda
MAP G1 ■ Alameda Dom Afonso Henriques, Avenida Almirante Reis

Alameda's narrow common and its monumental lighted fountain offer a glimpse of Lisbon as it was before 1974.

Restaurants and Cafés

1 Laurentina
MAP F1 ▪ Avenida Conde de
Valbom 71A ▪ 217 960 260 ▪ Closed
Sun ▪ €€

The self-proclaimed "King of
Cod" offers an exhaustive range of
bacalhau dishes, along with some
meatier options such as pork loin.

2 Ribadouro
MAP K1 ▪ Avenida da
Liberdade 155 ▪ 213 549 411 ▪ €€

This is one of the city's best
cervejarias (beer halls). Like many,
it specializes in seafood, although
some dishes are a little pricey.

3 Enoteca LX
MAP J2 ▪ Rua da Mãe d'Água
▪ 913 962 868 ▪ €€

The city's most appealing wine bar
serves tasty small dishes to go with
its wide choice of wines.

4 Psi
MAP G3 ▪ Alameda Santo
António dos Capuchos, Jardim dos
Sabores ▪ 213 590 573 ▪ Closed Sun
▪ €

This vegetarian and vegan restaurant
serves dishes from around the world
in a pleasant garden setting.

5 SushiCafé Avenida
MAP F3 ▪ Rua Barata Salgueiro
28 ▪ 211 928 158 ▪ Closed Sun ▪ €€

One of Lisbon's top Japanese
restaurants, SushiCafé specializes
in molecular cuisine. Black cod is
a favourite ingredient.

6 Café Mexicana
MAP G1 ▪ Avenida Guerra
Junqueiro 30 ▪ €€

This busy café and restaurant in the
Guerra Junqueiro/Roma shopping
area provides a neat slice of middle-
class Lisbon life, along with coffee
and ample pastries. The 1960s
interior has a certain appeal.

7 Eleven
MAP E2 ▪ Rua Marquês e
Fronteira, Jardim Amália Rodrigues
▪ 213 862 211 ▪ Closed Sun ▪ €€€

Lisbon's premier gourmet restaurant
that offers modern Mediterranean
food by Joachim Koerper, which has
earned it a Michelin star *(see p53)*.

Eleven's sophisticated interior

8 Portugália
MAP M2 ▪ Avenida Almirante
Reis 117 ▪ €€

The original – and most would say
best – branch of this popular chain.
Renowned for its seafood, it also
does good steaks and *pregos*
(steak sandwiches).

9 Choupana Caffé
MAP F2 ▪ Avenida da
República 25A

Just a few blocks from the Museu
Calouste Gulbenkian *(see pp30–31)*,
this café serves a staple Portuguese
breakfast and light snacks. Specialities
include savoury and sweet croissants.

10 Pastelaria Versailles
MAP F1 ▪ Avenida República
15A ▪ €€

Wonderful if slightly yellowed,
this café and patisserie has a
grandiose interior, attentive waiters
and worldly-wise elderly customers.

See map on p94

🔟 The Lisbon Coast

Coastline around Sintra

Its Riviera-rivalling heyday may be a distant memory now, but the varied coastline from the mouth of the Tejo to mainland Europe's westernmost point has other attractions too. Known locally as the *linha*, the coastal region has become one of Lisbon's most populous suburban zones – and yet it retains a laid-back holiday atmosphere. Above and behind it, Sintra's rock-strewn slopes and fragrant woods have a much more ancient ambience.

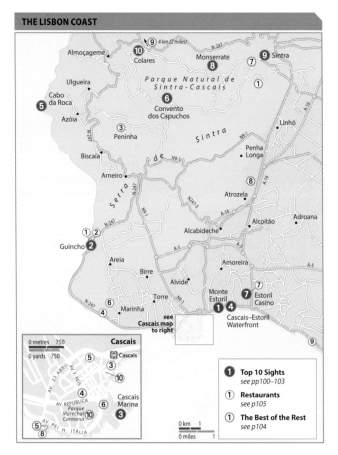

THE LISBON COAST

Top 10 Sights
see pp100–103

Restaurants
see p105

The Best of the Rest
see p104

1 Monte Estoril

The ridge that separates Estoril from Cascais was the site of the earliest resort development, during the first half of the 20th century. It is now a captivating jumble of grand mansions, shopping arcades and apartment hotels – and still manages to be leafy and quiet in parts. Its railway station is reached by way of a tunnel under the busy *Marginal* coast road.

2 Guincho

Still relatively undeveloped, the windswept coastline beyond Cascais, extending to Cabo da Roca, is exhilarating and scenic, particularly at Guincho. The beach of the same name is popular for surfing (although not recommended for beginners), and the broad sands are good for other beach sports and brisk walks. When it's too windy to swim or sunbathe, head for one of several smaller, more protected beaches on either side. Some of the best restaurants in the area lie along the Guincho road *(see p105)*.

Cascais marina at sunset

3 Cascais Marina

Casa de São Bernardo ▪ 214 824 800 ▪ Apr–Sep: 8:30am–8pm daily; Oct–Mar: 9am–6pm daily ▪ www.marinacascais.com

Just beyond the centre of town, and curving around the original fortress on the headland, Cascais Marina has 650 berths and can accommodate yachts up to 36 m (118 ft) long, with a maximum draught of 6 m (20 ft). The many small shops and restaurants also attract a non-sailing crowd. Nearby are the large municipal park of Cascais and the Museu Condes de Castro Guimarães *(see p104)*.

4 Cascais–Estoril Waterfront

Estoril and Cascais are linked by a long promenade that runs just above the beach, but mostly out of sight of the coast road. By far the best walk in either resort, the promenade is lined with small restaurants and bars and occasionally sprayed by Atlantic breakers.

Cascais town and beachfront

⑤ Cabo da Roca

The westernmost point of mainland Europe is a suitably dramatic clifftop location marked by a lighthouse. Also here is a quotation from Luís de Camões' epic poem *The Lusiads*, carved in stone. The cape is subject to the climatic peculiarities of the whole Sintra region, so take a jumper, even if it's hot when you leave Cascais; temperatures can be 10 degrees lower here, and winds strong. Collectors of memorabilia can buy a certificate to prove that they have walked on the continent's western extremity. There is a good café and restaurant, Moinho Dom Quixote, near the Sintra road turn-off, and Ursa beach *(see p45)* lies just north.

Clifftop Cabo da Roca

⑥ Convento dos Capuchos

On road EN247-3 ■ Open 9am–6pm daily ■ Adm ■ www.parquesdesintra.pt

Standing above Cabo da Roca, near Peninha *(see p104)*, this 16th-century Franciscan monastery is a striking example of monastic frugality, and thus a rarity among Portugal's generally opulent religious buildings. The Capuchin monks' cells are small and plain, hewn from rock and lined with cork against echoes and the cold. The minimal decoration is limited to communal areas such as the chapel, the refectory and the chapterhouse.

COLARES WINE

Once famous for its velvety, long-lived red wines made from the Ramisco grape – one of Europe's few survivors of the phylloxera plague – Colares seems now to be relegated to wine history. Wine is still made, but very little has any of the qualities associated with classic Colares. It seems that the costs of maintaining the old vines – and of planting new ones deep in the sand that protected them from the scourge of the vine louse – is too high.

⑦ Estoril Casino

Avenida Dr Stanley Ho ■ 214 667 700 ■ Open 3pm–3am daily ■ Adm varies ■ www.casino-estoril.pt

Large and rather loud in style, the entertainment heart of Estoril is more than just "Europe's biggest casino", offering both gaming tables and slot machines. It has several good restaurants, an art gallery, a varied concert calendar, a glitzy disco, a theatre stage and titillating floor shows. The palm-lined park in front adds a welcome touch of old-world glamour.

⑧ Monserrate

These lovely gardens, with their blend of natural and artificial elements, the unusual and the familiar, epitomize some of the essential characteristics of the Sintra region. The artificial "ruin" in the lower garden might have been designed for Walt Disney's *The Jungle Book*, and the rolling lawns are flanked by tropical trees and plants. The Palace

Monserrate Gardens and Palace

(see p32), renovated in 1858 by English nobleman Sir Francis Cook, represents a wonderful pastiche of Portuguese, Arabian and Indian architectural styles.

Palácio Nacional de Sintra

9 Sintra
To have seen the world and left out Sintra is not truly to have seen – thus goes, more or less, a Portuguese saying. When you visit this stunning hill town, set on the northern slopes of the Serra, it's easy to understand why it was the preferred summer retreat of Portuguese kings *(see pp32–3)*.

10 Colares
This peaceful village between Sintra and the sea gave its name to one of Portugal's most famous table wines, now made in only tiny amounts of variable quality. (Wine-lovers can visit the cooperative in Colares, at the beginning of the road to Praia das Maçãs, or go out to Adega Viúva Gomes *(www.adegaviuvagomes.com)*, a few miles east from Praia da Adraga. All the same, it's well worth lingering in the older parts of Colares, shaded by plane trees with their peeling, mottled bark. For something different, head to Flores do Cabo at Estrada dos Capuchos 839, a contemporary art gallery with an organic food restaurant.

A SINTRA DRIVE

▶ MORNING

Starting out from **Cascais** *(see p101)*, drive along the Guincho coast towards Cabo da Roca (road N247). After Guincho beach, the road begins to climb. Follow the main road past the turning to Malveira da Serra. Turn off to the left for **Cabo da Roca** or, a tiny bit further on, to the right for **Peninha** *(see p104)* and **Convento dos Capuchos**. The latter offers opportunities for walks in the woods and views across the Serra; the former an invigorating lungful of sea air and the possibility of a drink at **Moinho Dom Quixote**. Carry on towards **Colares** and stop there for lunch, taking time to explore the village.

AFTERNOON

From Colares take the smaller N375 road heading inland towards Sintra, which will lead you past Eugaria and to **Monserrate**. Make an extended stop at Monserrate, giving yourself time to enjoy the gardens. Carry on along the lovely road that tunnels through the woods until you reach stately **Seteais** *(see p117)*, where tea might be in order. A short distance further on you will come to **Quinta da Regaleira** *(see p32)* – worth visiting for its gardens and esoterica – before you enter **Sintra** proper. Follow the road up, until you find parking above the main town, then walk down and do the sights or head straight to **Lawrence's** *(see p116)* for dinner. You can return to Cascais (and Lisbon) via the faster N9.

See map on p100 ←

The Best of the Rest

Parque da Pena and the Palácio

1 Parque da Pena
N247-3 ■ Park: open 9am–7pm daily; Palace: open 9:30am–6:30pm daily ■ Adm

The paths in the park around the Palácio da Pena lead to the highest point in the Sintra hills – Cruz Alta, at 530 m (1,740 ft).

2 Golf courses
www.penhalonga.com; www.oitavosdunes.com

There are eight golf courses along the Lisbon coast. Penha Longa, between Cascais and Sintra, and Oitavos, in the Quinta da Marinha complex, are the best places to play.

3 Peninha
N247

The Capela de Nossa Senhora de Penha was built at the turn of the 17th century. In 1918 António Carvalho Monteiro, millionaire owner of the Quinta da Regaleira (see p32), added a mock-fortified eagle's-nest residence.

4 Casa das Histórias Paula Rego
Avenida da República 300, Cascais ■ 214 826 970 ■ Open 10am–6pm Tue–Sun ■ Adm

Celebrated here are the works of the artist Paula Rego, known for depictions of folk tales and strong female types.

5 Boca do Inferno
Estrada da Boca do Inferno (N247-8)

The rocky coastline beyond Cascais is full of crevices cut by the waves.

The "Mouth of Hell" is a particularly deep one, where the waves roar in and then shoot up a vertical hole.

6 Cidadela de Cascais
Avenida D. Carlos I

The 16th-century ramparts of this fortress enclose several upmarket boutiques and art galleries, as well as a *pousada* which houses the Taberna da Praça restaurant.

7 Palácio Biester
Avenida Almeida Garrett 1A ■ Open 10am–8pm daily (to 6:30pm Nov–Mar) ■ Closed 1 Jan & 25 Dec ■ Adm ■ www.biester.pt

This 19th-century palace opened to the public for the first time in 2022. The surrounding park offers views of Sintra's top attractions.

8 Autódromo do Estoril
N9, Alcabideche

The Formula 1 Portuguese Grand Prix was held at Estoril's racetrack from 1984 to 1996. Today it hosts MotoGP and A1 Grand Prix events.

9 Azenhas do Mar
N375

This clifftop village spills down towards a rock pool by the Atlantic ocean. With several restaurants, it is popular for Sunday lunch outings.

Azenhas do Mar, above a rock pool

10 Museu Condes de Castro Guimarães
Avenida Rei Humberto II de Itália ■ 214 815 301 ■ 10am–1pm & 2–6pm Tue–Sun ■ Adm

This tower and grand villa on a small creek just beyond Cascais marina (see p101) are said to have been inspired by a painting.

Restaurants

PRICE CATEGORIES

For a three-course meal for one with half a bottle of wine (or equivalent meal), taxes and extra charges.

€ under €20   €€ €20–€40   €€€ over €40

 1 Fortaleza do Guincho
Estrada do Guincho, Cascais
■ 214 870 491 ■ Closed Tue–Sat L;
Sun & Mon ■ €€€

Magnificently sited in a 17th-century fortress, this Michelin-starred restaurant has modern French à la carte and tasting menus that feature Portuguese ingredients.

2 Porto de Santa Maria
Estrada do Guincho ■ 214 879 450 ■ €€€

Set in a low, modern building across the dramatic coastline near Guincho beach, this is one of the country's top fish and seafood restaurants.

3 Masala
Rua Frederico Arouca 288
■ 214 865 334 ■ €€

An informal restaurant, with a good selection of Indian dishes, including many vegetarian options.

4 Dom Grelhas, Cascais
Casa da Guia, Estrada do Guincho ■ 918 500 782 ■ Closed Tue ■ €€

Located in a gated huddle of restaurants and shops, Dom Grelhas specializes in grilled meat and fish.

5 O Pereira, Cascais
Travessa da Bela Vista 42, Cascais ■ 214 831 215 ■ €

This small, friendly restaurant serves hearty Portuguese food.

6 Verbasco, Cascais
Quinta da Marinha Oitavos Golf ■ 214 860 606 ■ Closed D daily; Mon ■ €€

Sophisticated modern cuisine is served here in the airy clubhouse of the Oitavos golf course.

7 Estoril Mandarim
Casino do Estoril ■ 214 667 270
■ Closed Mon, Tue ■ €€

Part of the Casino complex in Estoril, this is Portugal's most luxurious and also its best Chinese restaurant. From their extensive menu, try the Peking roast duck and the dim sums.

Elegant decor at Estoril Mandarim

8 Mar do Inferno
Avenida Rei Humberto II de Itália ■ 214 832 218 ■ Closed Wed ■ €€€

With the Boca do Inferno at its feet, this restaurant offers splendid coastal views paired with fresh fish and seafood platters. There are dishes for two people which mix both options.

9 Bar das Avencas
Avenida Marginal, Parede
■ 214 572 717 ■ Closed Tue in winter ■ €

Seemingly hanging off the cliff above a quiet beach, this simple but nicely designed bar offers a menu of sandwiches, salads and hamburgers, plus a couple of similarly unfussy cooked dishes.

10 O Pescador, Cascais
Rua das Flores 10B, Cascais
■ 214 832 054 ■ Closed Wed ■ €€

Nautical memorabilia adorns the walls of this restaurant, which specializes in fresh seafood. The wine cellar is one of the best stocked in the region.

See map on p100

Streetsmart

Statue of poet Fernando Pessoa outside A Brasileira café in Chiado

Getting Around

Arriving by Air

Humberto Delgado Airport, on the northern outskirts of Lisbon, is served by local and international flights. A taxi to the centre costs €15–18 and takes 20–30 minutes (double during rush hour). The easiest way to reach the city by public transport is via the metro. Take the red line from the airport until Alameda (nine stops), then change to the green line. Central stops include Rossio, Baixa-Chiado and Cais do Sodré. The journey takes around 35 minutes. You can also take buses 705, 722, 744 and 783, but it will be harder to carry luggage onboard. Single tickets for both services cost €1.50 (€2 if purchased on the bus).

Train Travel

There are two main routes into Portugal by train. The Sud Express – departing daily at 6:45pm from Irun on the French-Spanish border – can be reached from Austerlitz station in Paris. Alternatively, the overnight train from Madrid takes 10 hours. Both routes are operated by the Spanish state-run service **Renfe**.

Most parts of Portugal are served by rail, with trains operated by **Comboios de Portugal**. Lisbon has four main train stations: Rossio, Cais do Sodré, Santa Apolónia and Oriente. Rossio and Cais do Sodré cover local journeys with lines to Sintra and Cascais respectively. Santa Apolónia and Oriente provide links to international destinations and those across Portugal.

Long-Distance Bus Travel

Most national and international buses arrive at the main city bus station at Sete Rios. The main national coach carrier is **Rede Expressos**, which has regular services to most towns and cities throughout the country. Flixbus also runs regional trips, as well as international connections with Spain and France.

Driving to Lisbon

You can arrive from the north on the A1, which passes Lisbon. From the south and east, drivers arrive on the A2 motorway via the 25 de Abril toll bridge. Alternatively, take the A12, which branches off the A2 just after Setúbal and leads to the Vasco da Gama toll bridge, the best approach for the north and east of the city via the airport.

Most car hire firms have offices at the airport and in central locations, as well as on the coast. Reputable companies include Avis, Europcar and Hertz. Drivers must show a valid licence and be aged at least 21. European and US driving licences are valid.

Public Transport

Carris is the city's main public transport authority and is responsible for buses, trams and elevators. The metro is run separately. Safety and hygiene measures, timetables, ticket information and maps can be found online, on the Carris app and inside some stations.

The Lisboa MOVE-ME app is very useful for navigating the city's public transport. The Citymapper app, meanwhile, covers all urban modes of transport.

Metro and Bus

Covering most of the city, apart from the west, the modern **Metropolitano de Lisboa** is the fastest and cheapest way of getting around. Buy tickets at machines by the entrance or at the kiosks. Trains run from 6:30am to 1am.

Buses run to all parts of the city and are generally reliable, though subject to traffic conditions. Usually yellow, they generally run from 5:30am to 1am in the inner city. A small number of night services continue outside these hours.

Trams and Funiculars

Trams are a pleasant way of sightseeing but they only operate in limited areas of the city. The most useful trams for exploring are the 28, which runs from Alfama to Prazeres in the west via the historic centre, and the 25, which runs parallel to the riverfront and serves the area west of the centre.

Three historic funiculars (Glória, Bica and Lavra) carry weary Lisboetas up several of the city's steepest hills. The Elevador de

Santa Justa is an enjoyable tourist experience, but queues can be long.

Ferries

The frequent commuter ferries over the Tagus, which depart roughly every 15 minutes, make for a fun excursion to the port suburb of Cacilhas. Most ferry services are run by **Transtejo** and depart regularly from Cais do Sodré, Terreiro do Paço and Belém to several destinations south of the river.

Tickets

Single-trip paper tickets for buses, funiculars and trams can be bought upon boarding. Multitrip paper tickets have been replaced with electronic passes, such as the **Navegante** smart card. Costing €0.50, these cards can be topped up whenever necessary or loaded with a 24-hour pass, which allows unlimited travel with Carris and on the metro for €6.45. Cards are sold at ticket offices in metro stations and vending machines, plus some railway stations, shops and newsagents.

Driving in Lisbon

Lisbon's central streets are narrow and congested, so driving is not recommended. There are several car parks, as well as metered on-street parking.

Taxis

Lisbon's taxis are relatively inexpensive compared to the rest of Europe and can work out cheaper than public transport for large groups. Taxis can be hailed in the street and at taxi ranks. A green light indicates that the taxi is available and two green lights mean a higher rate. The normal starting rate is €3.25 during the day and €3.90 at night. Ensure that the meter is on, agree on a price for longer routes and check the extra cost for luggage before setting off. Note that most drivers only accept cash. **Cooptáxis** and **Retalis Radio Taxis** have large fleets of cabs. Taxi apps such as Uber also operate.

Walking

Wandering around Lisbon's pretty streets is one of the most enjoyable aspects of the city, and the main sights are generally within walking distance. However, its hilly streets are steep, making them tough going – especially in hot weather – and slippery in the rain.

Lisbon Walker provides informative and fun walking tours, which vary from walks around the old town to themed walks. Other good walking tours include the **African Lisbon Tour** *(see p69)* and the **Devour Lisbon Food Tour**.

Cycling

Lisbon's hilly terrain does not make for easy cycling, but cycle paths do exist. The vast Monsanto Forest Park can provide quieter roads and respite from the sun, while there are several popular cycle routes south of the river. A growing number of companies, including **Lisbon Bike Rentals**, now offer electric bikes. Other hire companies include **Belém Bike** and **Gira**.

DIRECTORY

ARRIVING BY AIR

Humberto Delgado Airport
w ana.pt

TRAIN TRAVEL

Comboios de Portugal
w cp.pt

Renfe
w renfe.com

LONG-DISTANCE BUS TRAVEL

Flixbus
w global.flixbus.com

Rede Expressos
w rede-expressos.pt

PUBLIC TRANSPORT

Carris
w carris.pt

METRO AND BUS

Metropolitano de Lisboa
w metrolisboa.pt

FERRIES

Transtejo
w ttsl.pt

TICKETS

Navegante
w www.navegante.pt

TAXIS

Cooptáxis
w cooptaxis.pt

Retalis Radio Taxis
w retalis.pt

WALKING

African Lisbon Tour
w africanlisbontour.com

Devour Lisbon Food Tour
w devourlisbonfoodtours.com

Lisbon Walker
w lisbonwalker.com

CYCLING

Belém Bike
w biclas.com

Gira
w gira-bicicletasdelisboa.pt

Lisbon Bike Rentals
w lisbonbikerentals.com

Practical Information

Passports and Visas

For entry requirements, including visas, consult your nearest Portuguese embassy or check the Portuguese **Ministry of Foreign Affairs**. From late 2023, citizens of the UK, US, Canada, Australia and New Zealand do not need a visa for stays of up to three months, but must apply in advance for the European Travel Information and Authorization System (**ETIAS**). Visitors from other countries may also require an ETIAS, so check before travelling. EU nationals do not need a visa or an ETIAS.

Government Advice

Now more than ever, it is important to consult both your and the Portuguese government's advice before travelling. The **UK Foreign, Commonwealth & Development Office (FCDO)**, the **US State Department**, the **Australian Department of Foreign Affairs and Trade** and the **Câmara Municipal de Lisboa** offer the latest information on security, health and local regulations.

Customs Information

You can find information on the laws relating to goods and currency taken in or out of Portugal on the **Visit Portugal** website.

For EU citizens, there are no limits on goods that can be taken into or out of Portugal, provided they are for your personal use.

Insurance

We recommend that you take out a comprehensive insurance policy covering theft, loss of belongings, medical care, cancellations and delays, and read the small print carefully.

UK citizens are eligible for free emergency medical care in Portugal provided they have a valid European Health Insurance Card (**EHIC**) or UK Global Health Insurance Card (**GHIC**). All other nationalities should make sure to take out private health insurance.

Health

Portugal has a world-class health system. Emergency medical care is free for all EU citizens. If you have an EHIC, present this as soon as possible. You may have to pay after treatment and reclaim the money later.

For other visitors, payment of medical expenses is the patient's responsibility. It is therefore important to arrange comprehensive medical insurance beforehand.

No inoculations are necessary for Portugal. Unless stated otherwise, tap water is safe to drink.

Seek medicinal supplies and advice for minor ailments from pharmacies (*farmácias*), identifiable by a green cross. Pharmacists can dispense a range of drugs that would normally be available only on prescription in many other countries. A closed pharmacy will have a sign in its window listing one that is open nearby.

For more serious problems or emergencies, there are several central public and private hospitals. The largest central hospital is **Hospital de Santa Maria**.

Smoking, Alcohol and Drugs

Smoking is banned in most enclosed public spaces and is a fineable offence, although some bars still allow it.

Portugal has a high alcohol consumption rate, however it is frowned upon to be openly drunk. It is common for locals to drink on the street outside the bar of purchase.

All drugs are decriminalized in Portugal, but possession of small quantities is considered a public health issue and results in a warning or small fine. Drug-dealers brazenly plying their wares in the city centre can be a small nuisance but pose no threat.

ID

By law you must carry ID with you at all times. A photocopy of your passport should suffice. If stopped by the police you may be asked to report to a police station with the original document.

Personal Security

Lisbon is a relatively safe city to visit, where you only really need to be wary of pickpockets. Take care in crowded tourist areas and on popular tram routes, particularly the 28 and 15. Avoid leaving valuables in hired cars.

If you have anything stolen, report the crime within 24 hours to the nearest police station and take ID with you. Get a copy of the crime report to make an insurance claim. There is a police station specifically for tourists – run by the English-speaking **PSP Tourism Police** – at Praça dos Restauradores, beside the tourist office. Contact your embassy if you have your passport stolen, or in the event of a serious crime or accident.

All of the **Emergency Services** (police, fire service and ambulance) can be contacted by dialling 112.

As a rule, Lisboetas are very accepting of all people, regardless of their race, gender or sexuality. Homosexuality was legalized in 1982 and in 2010, Portugal became the eighth country in the world to recognize same-sex marriage. If you do feel unsafe, the **Safe Space Alliance** pinpoints your nearest place of refuge.

Women may receive unwanted and unwelcome attention around tourist areas. If you feel threatened, head straight to the nearest police station.

As in any city, be cautious when walking alone at night through quiet districts, taking care to always follow well-lit main streets.

Beware of currents and undertow at the city's Atlantic beaches, and don't ignore the safety flags: red – no going in the sea; yellow – no swimming; green – all clear. Nasty stings in shallow water may be from poisonous weever fish (peixe-aranha) buried in

the sand. Seek the help of a lifeguard or apply hot water to the area, which can alleviate the temporary intense pain and swelling.

Travellers with Specific Requirements

Lisbon's hills and narrow cobbled pavements (often with parked cars blocking the way) can prove a challenge for visitors with reduced mobility and those with prams. Facilities in Lisbon have improved, with wheelchairs, adapted toilets, and reserved car parking available at the city's airports and main stations. Ramps and lifts are installed in many public places and some buses (marked with a blue-and-white logo at the front) accommodate wheelchair-users.

Most sights offer audio guides. Some museums, including the Museu Nacional do Azulejo (see p26), offer free video guides in both Portuguese sign language and the International sign system. Others, such as the Museu Nacional dos Coches (see p88), have braille signs (but these are not as common).

Some tour companies, such as **Tourism For All**, offer specialist holiday packages adapted cars and equipment rentals, while **Accessible Portugal** gives comprehensive advice on travelling with limited mobility. The latter has created a website and app called **TUR4all** that promotes accessible tourism in Portugal. **Portugal 4All Senses**, meanwhile, organizes tours with the visually impaired in mind.

Time Zone

Portugal operates on Greenwich Mean Time (GMT), which is four hours ahead of EST. Clocks go forward an hour in late March and back to GMT in late October.

Money

Portugal is one of the European countries using the euro (€). Major credit cards are widely accepted in bigger hotels, shops, restaurants and bars. Contactless payments are gradually becoming more common in Lisbon, but it's always a good idea to carry cash for smaller items like coffee and *pastéis de nata*, or when visiting markets or hailing a taxi. The easiest way to withdraw money is using ATMs, known as Multibanco, which are widely available across the city. Nearly all accept debit and credit cards from the major card companies, but transaction charges will apply.

Banks can also be used to change money. For the less common currencies, and outside of banking hours, seek out one of the Forex services in Rossio and Praça da Figueira.

Tipping around 10 per cent is normal when dining out or travelling by taxi; hotel porters and house-keeping will expect €1-2 per bag or day.

Electrical Appliances

Portugal uses two-pin plugs (220–240 volts). You will need an adaptor, and possibly a transformer (for some US appliances).

Mobile Phones and Wi-Fi

Most mobile phones have good connections throughout Lisbon. Visitors travelling to Portugal with EU tariffs are able to use their devices abroad without being affected by roaming charges. Users will be charged the same rates for data, calls and texts as at home. The country code is 351.

Free Wi-Fi is widespread in the city's restaurants, cafés and bars, specifically those aimed at tourists.

Postal Services

Correios (post offices) are dotted around the city. For buying stamps, it is more convenient to use the red, coin-operated dispensers, which will save you queuing. Express mail is known as *correio azul*.

The main post office on Restauradores is open on weekdays and some sections operate on Saturday morning; most other post offices operate 9am–6pm on weekdays only.

Weather

Lisbon is one of Europe's sunniest capitals, so you can expect sunshine year-round. Spring and autumn are probably the best times to visit, with warm temperatures (and fewer crowds), though you should expect the odd shower. June to October is usually clear and hot, with temperatures peaking in July and August. Being on the Atlantic means that the city also gets plenty of rainfall and winter flooding is not uncommon.

Opening Hours

Banks are open from 8:30am to 3pm Monday to Friday. Shop hours are from 9am to 1pm and from 2 or 3pm to 7pm on weekdays. Shops are generally open until lunchtime on Saturday and closed on Sunday. Large shopping centres are an exception, with many outlets staying open all day, every day, until 11pm or midnight.

Most museums and monuments are open Tuesday to Sunday 9:30am–6pm (often later in summer); check individual websites for specific times.

Restaurants usually open for lunch around noon to 3pm and for dinner from 7 to 11:30pm.

The COVID-19 pandemic proved that situations can change suddenly. Always check before visiting attractions and hospitality venues for up-to-date hours and booking requirements.

Visitor Information

Both the official Visit Portugal (*see p110*) and **Visit Lisboa** websites contain useful information for visitors to the city.

The city's main tourist office is the **Lisbon Welcome Centre** on the riverfront Praça do Comércio. There is also an office in **Palácio Foz** in Praça dos Restauradores, which has information for

Portugal as a whole. Smaller offices can often be found at train stations and at the Humberto Delgado Airport (see p108), while Ask Me information kiosks are dotted round the city.

If you plan to pack a lot of sightseeing into a short trip, purchasing an official **Lisboa Card** can be a cost-efficient choice. For €21, adults receive 24 hours of free public transport, which includes the train lines to Cascais and Sintra; free entry to 26 museums and points of interest; and discounts relating to tours, shopping and nightlife. Cards lasting 48 and 72 hours are also available (€35/€44). The cards can be bought online, at the airport and in the tourist offices at Praça do Comércio and Praça dos Restauradores.

The Agenda Cultural website lists monthly events, as does the tourist association's monthly *Follow Me Lisboa* magazine. Art-lovers can also download the excellent Street Art Cities app, which provides information on the location of Lisbon's street art.

Visiting Churches and Cathedrals

Most churches and cathedrals will not permit visitors during Sunday Mass. Visit any other time and day and entrance is generally free, however a fee may apply to enter special areas, such as cloisters or crypts. Portugal retains a strong Catholic identity. When visiting religious buildings ensure that

you are dressed modestly, with your knees and shoulders covered.

Language

Portuguese is the official language in Lisbon. English is widely spoken, but locals very much appreciate visitors' efforts to communicate in the Portuguese language.

Taxes and Refunds

VAT is usually 23 per cent. Under certain conditions, non-EU citizens can claim a rebate. Either claim the rebate before you buy (show your passport to the shop assistant and complete a form) or claim it retrospectively by presenting a customs officer with your receipts as you leave.

Accommodation

Lisbon offers a wide variety of accommodation, ranging from boutique hotels to campsites, budget hostels to private apartment rentals.

There are plenty of hotel options in and around the centre, among them simple three-star hotels and luxury places. Lisbon also has many inexpensive guesthouses, traditionally known as *pensões* or *residenciais*, but now officially called *alojamentos locais*. These are often in traditional buildings in good locations and usually offer en-suite facilities. Be aware that front-facing rooms can be very noisy. The city is tackling noise pollution with a hotline set up for antisocial noise complaints.

Lisbon has a number of hostels, including official youth hostels and some excellent privately run places. These often have double and family rooms as well as dorms.

There are a few options for self-catering stays, ranging from characterful apartments in the historic Alfama quarter to plush studios in the suburbs.

An extensive list of accommodation can be found on the Visit Portugal website (see p111).

During the summer months, lodgings are snapped up fast and prices become inflated, so book in advance. Lisbon is a popular short citybreak destination, and it can also be difficult to find a last-minute weekend booking during the low season (Dec–Mar).

Visitors to Lisbon are required to pay a €2/night city tourism tax for stays up to 7 days, which is payable on top of your bill. Children below the age of 13 are exempt. Hotels are required by law to share details of foreign visitors with the local authorities.

DIRECTORY

VISITOR INFORMATION
Lisboa Card
🌐 shop.visitlisboa.com/ pt/products/lisboa-card
Lisbon Welcome Centre
MAP M5 ◼ Praça do Comércio/ Rua do Arsenal 15
📞 914 081 366
Palácio Foz
MAP L2 ◼ Praça dos Restauradores
📞 213 463 314
Visit Lisboa
🌐 visitlisboa.com

Places to Stay

PRICE CATEGORIES

For a standard double room per night (with breakfast if included), taxes and extra charges.

€ under 100   €€ €100–€250   €€€ over €250

Luxury Hotels

Heritage Avenida Liberdade

MAP F3 ▪ Avenida da Liberdade 28 ▪ 213 404 040 ▪ www.heritage.pt ▪ €€

Part of the small Heritage hotel group, this centrally located hotel occupies a restored late 18th-century building. Portuguese architect Miguel Câncio Martins has retained the building's original features, complementing them with a simple, modern boutique-style interior.

Palácio do Governador

MAP A6 ▪ Rua Bartolomeu Dias 117 ▪ 213 007 009 ▪ www.palacio governador.com ▪ €€

Housed in an attractively restored historic building in the tourist centre of Belém, this exquisite hotel has a gourmet restaurant and a spa.

Real Palácio

MAP F2 ▪ Rua Tomás Ribeiro 115 ▪ 213 199 500 ▪ www.real hotelsgroup.com ▪ €€

Old and new Lisbon come together here. A restored private palace, dating back to the 17th century in its oldest parts, adjoins a modern hotel building. It is the palace, with its small patio, archways and tiled stairwells, that is the highlight.

Sofitel Lisbon Liberdade

MAP K1 ▪ Avenida da Liberdade 127 ▪ 213 228 300 ▪ www.sofitel-lisbon-liberdade.com ▪ €€

Ideally placed near Lisbon's commercial district and close to the main sights, the stylish Sofitel is popular with business executives for its modern facilities.

Avenida Palace

MAP L3 ▪ Rua 1 de Dezembro 123 ▪ 213 218 100 ▪ www.hotel avenidapalace.pt ▪ €€€

The doyen of the city's luxury hotels has a colourful history going back to the early 20th century. It has undergone a major restoration but retains its traditional *belle époque* style.

Olissippo Lapa Palace

MAP E5 ▪ Rua do Pau de Bandeira 4 ▪ 213 949 494 ▪ www.olissippo hotels.com ▪ €€€

Opulent and eclectic in its decor, this hotel, overlooking the Tagus River, is an established jewel in Lisbon's crown. The location is quiet, but quite a walk from the centre.

Pestana Palace

MAP C5 ▪ Rua Jau 54 ▪ 213 615 600 ▪ www. pestana.com ▪ €€€

Occupying a marvellously restored 19th-century palace with views of the Tejo, this grand hotel has more modern extensions framing a garden. It is located between central Lisbon and Belém.

Pousada de Lisboa

MAP M5 ▪ Praça do Comércio 31–34 ▪ 210 407 640 ▪ www. pousadas.pt ▪ €€€

Housed in the former Ministry of Internal Affairs, right on the riverfront Praça do Comércio, this *pousada* combines tradition and modern flair. Plush, elegant rooms, many overlooking the river, are complemented by a sauna, spa, swimming pool, two bars and an excellent restaurant.

Ritz Four Seasons

MAP F3 ▪ Rua Rodrigo da Fonseca 88 ▪ 213 811 400 ▪ www.fourseasons.com/lisbon ▪ €€€

From the outside, the Ritz Four Seasons perhaps isn't much, but it offers charterful interiors and excellent facilities, including a rooftop running track with amazing view of the city. Most importantly, the Ritz provides wonderful hospitality and is absolutely dedicated to its guests.

Character Hotels

Bairro Alto

MAP K4 ▪ Praça Luís de Camões 2 ▪ 213 408 288 ▪ www.bairroaltohotel. com ▪ €€€

Set in an attractively restored 18th-century building in Praça de Camões, in the heart of Lisbon, this hotel delivers luxury with style.

Britânia

MAP F3 ■ Rua Rodrigues Sampaio 17 ■ 213 155 016 ■ www.heritage.pt ■ €€
Situated in a quiet street just off Avenida da Liberdade, the Britânia is housed in a 1940s building, which combines wood and marble in a glorious restoration of its original Art Deco design. Rooms are sleek, tasteful and modern.

Inspira Liberdade Boutique

MAP F3 ■ Rua de Santa Marta 48 ■ 210 440 900 ■ www.inspirahotels.com ■ €€
Designed (according to Feng Shui principles) as an urban retreat, the four-star Inspira Liberdade Boutique combines a 19th- century façade with an eye-catching minimalist interior. It is committed to sustainability.

Solar do Castelo

MAP N3 ■ Rua das Cozinhas 2 ■ 218 806 050 ■ www.lisbonheritage hotels.com/solar-do-castelo ■ €€€
Once the kitchens of the original Alcáçovas Palace in Castelo de São Jorge (see pp12–13), then converted into a private palace in the 18th century, this is now a cosy, eclectically furnished boutique hotel, with rooms around a small courtyard.

Memmo Alfama

MAP P4 ■ Travessa das Merceeiras 27 ■ 210 495 660 ■ www.memmo hotels.com ■ €€€
The first boutique hotel to make an appearance in the historic Alfama district, this has a range of tastefully furnished rooms hidden behind the façade of a gorgeous 19th-century building. You'll also find a wine bar, pool and terrace offering dazzling views across the Tejo estuary.

Palacete Chafariz d'El Rei

MAP H4 ■ Travessa do Chafariz de El-Rei 6 ■ 218 886 150 ■ www.chafariz delrei.com ■ €€€
Six elegant suites, each with its own character, are available at this eclectic 19th-century palace. The building is a mix of Neo-Moorish and Art Nouveau elements, carefully maintained over the years. Tucked away in the Alfama neighbourhood, Chafariz d'El Rei offers a cosy library and a luxurious restaurant.

Budget Hotels

Bairro Alto Suites

MAP K2 ■ Rua da Rosa 252 ■ 966 405 844 ■ www. bairroaltosuites.com ■ €
Located in Bairro Alto, this minimalist hotel is an economical choice, and very close to the cocktail bar Pavilhão Chinês (see p82). Its comfortable rooms include balconies with city views.

Independente

MAP K3 ■ Rua São Pedro de Alcântara 81 ■ 213 461 381 ■ www.theindependente.pt ■ Dorms €, rooms €€
Part hostel and part quirky hotel, all the rooms here are inside a beautifully restored former mansion. There's a bar and breakfast room, and the adjacent Independente Suites & Terrace has more rooms and a rooftop restaurant.

Home Lisbon Hostel

MAP H4 ■ Rua de São Nicolau 13 ■ 218 885 312 ■ www.homelisbon hostel.com ■ €
This friendly hostel is conveniently located near Rua Augusta. It has a welcoming living-room-style lounge, a bar and a communal kitchen, where homemade meals are prepared daily. Breakfast is included.

Londres

MAP K2 ■ Rua Dom Pedro V 53, 2 ■ 213 462 203 ■ www.pensaolondres. com.pt ■ €
Longtime favourite of budget travellers, the Londres has gone upmarket. Cheaper rooms are still available, but the best one is at the top, overlooking Bairro Alto's warren of streets.

Selina Secret Garden

MAP F4 ■ Beco Carrasco 1 ■ 937 532 538 ■ www. selina.com/portugal/secret-garden-lisbon ■ €
One of a new breed of high-quality hostels that also offers good-value double rooms. Traveller's House couldn't be more central, occupying a traditional town house on Lisbon's main street.

Florescente

MAP L2 ■ Rua Portas de Santo Antão 99 ■ 213 426 609 ■ www.residencial florescente.com ■ €€
This place feels grander than the price suggests. It is also neater than most of its competition. The central location, parking facilities and free Wi-Fi enhance the excellent value it offers. Some superior rooms have a small living room.

Rooms with a View

Albergaria Senhora do Monte
MAP P1 ▪ Calçada do Monte 39 ▪ 218 866 002 ▪ www.hotelsenhora monte.com ▪ €€
Set on one of Lisbon's highest hills, this relatively plain hotel has some of the city's best views. It's a quiet spot, and full of atmosphere.

Dom Pedro
MAP E3 ▪ Avenida Engenheiro Duarte Pacheco 24 ▪ 213 896 600 ▪ www.dompedro.com ▪ €€
This lofty glass pile in the Amoreiras business and shopping district features a luxurious spa and traditionally styled interiors. There are stunning views across the Tejo from almost every room.

Mundial
MAP M3 ▪ Praça Martim Moniz 2 ▪ 218 842 000 ▪ www.hotel-mundial.pt ▪ €€
Superbly located in downtown Lisbon, the eight-floor Mundial has views that stretch across the Baixa and up towards the castle. Its comfortable rooms have large windows that open: a potential hazard for young children. The restaurant is popular with local dignitaries.

Sheraton
MAP F2 ▪ Rua Latino Coelho 1 ▪ 213 120 000 ▪ www.sheratonlisboa. com ▪ €€
A landmark on the city's modest skyline, the Sheraton has beautiful views and a modern interior. Primarily a business hotel, it offers five-star comfort at reasonable rates and a rooftop restaurant.

Solar dos Mouros
MAP N4 ▪ Rua do Milagre de Santo António 6 ▪ 218 854 940 ▪ www.solardos mouroslisboa.com ▪ €€
Built over the remains of one of the Moorish-era gates to Castelo de São Jorge, this small hotel has tastefully decorated rooms. Art from the owner's private collection features prominently, as do views of the city and the river.

Tryp Lisboa Oriente
MAP D1 ▪ Avenida Dom João II ▪ 218 930 000 ▪ www.tryporiente.com ▪ €€
This modern hotel by Parque das Nações (see pp20–21) offers views of the wide Tejo estuary from its airy rooms. Part of the Meliá Hotels chain, it is handy for the airport.

Altis Belém Hotel & Spa
MAP A6 ▪ Doca do Bom Sucesso ▪ 210 400 200 ▪ www.altishotels.com ▪ €€€
Lisbon's first five-star riverfront hotel still commands uninterrupted views of the Tejo. It's also noted for its cutting-edge interior design and its Michelin-starred restaurant, Feitoria.

Lisbon Coast Hotels

Fortaleza do Guincho
Estrada do Guincho, Cascais ▪ 214 870 491 ▪ www.fortalezado guincho.pt ▪ €€
Housed in an old fortress on a cliff by Guincho beach, this hotel has vaulted rooms and grand staircases. Best of all are the junior suites, with their arcaded terraces facing the Atlantic. The restaurant has one Michelin star.

Lawrence's
Rua Consigliéri Pedroso 38–40, Sintra ▪ 219 105 500 ▪ www.lawrences hotel.com ▪ €€
Dating from 1764, this charming hotel on the edge of Sintra town claims to be the oldest on the Iberian peninsula. Some of its individually furnished rooms are named after famous guests, among them Lord Byron.

Senhora da Guia
Estrada do Guincho, Cascais ▪ 214 869 239 ▪ www.senhoradaguia. com ▪ €€
Just outside central Cascais – and close to the Quinta da Marinha golf course – Senhora da Guia embodies civilized luxury. The hotel has a lovely salt-water swimming pool with an adjacent bar.

Albatroz
Rua Frederico Arouca 100, Cascais ▪ 214 847 380 ▪ www.thealbatroz collection.com ▪ €€€
Central Cascais' most characterful hotel has a to-die-for location on a promontory with sandy beaches to either side. The main building typifies the summer villas built here for aristocrats in the 19th century.

Farol Hotel
Avenida Rei Humberto II de Itália 7, Cascais ▪ 214 823 490 ▪ www. farol.com.pt ▪ €€€
Within an extended villa overlooking the

sea, this modern luxury hotel has interiors designed by top names in Portuguese fashion. For all the design hype, the main attraction is that some rooms have floor-to-ceiling windows, providing a unique bedtime experience.

Palácio Estoril
Rua Particular, Estoril ▪ 214 648 000 ▪ www.palacioestorilhotel.com ▪ €€€
Harking back to Estoril's heyday as a glamorous resort, the Palácio was built in the 1930s and former guests range from royalty to spies. Testament to its enduring grandeur are the hotel's interiors and impeccable service.

Palácio Seteais
Rua Barbosa du Bocage 8–10, Sintra ▪ 219 233 200 ▪ www.tivolihotels.com ▪ €€€
One of the many gems of the Sintra region, this palatial hotel was built in 1787; its Neo-Classical façade and triumphal arch were added later. Now part of the Tivoli chain, it offers all the usual luxuries and an inimitable atmosphere.

Self-catering, Family and Camping

Avenida Park
MAP F2 ▪ Avenida Sidónio Pais 6 ▪ 213 532 181 ▪ www.avenidapark.com ▪ €
Just off Parque Eduardo VII (see p95), this hotel offers good value, modern, simple rooms with large windows, and a practical location. Most rooms overlook the park.

Camping Orbitur, Costa da Caparica
Avda Afonso de Albuquerque, Quinta S António ▪ 212 901 366 ▪ www.orbitur.pt ▪ €
Situated near the northern end of the Caparica coast, this camp site set among pines is just 200 m (220 yards) from the beach. Many lisboetas have semi-permanent set-ups here, and it can get crowded in the summer.

Camping Orbitur, Guincho
Lugar de Areia, Cascais ▪ 214 870 450 ▪ www.orbitur.pt ▪ €
Attractively located among umbrella pines behind the dunes of Guincho beach, this campsite is popular with surfers. Among its facilities is a tennis court. Bungalows are available.

Lisboa Camping
MAP B3 ▪ Estrada Circunvalação ▪ 217 628 200 ▪ www.lisboacamping.com ▪ €
Lisbon's main campsite is located in the Monsanto park (see p86), immediately west of the centre. Well equipped in practical as well as leisure terms, it can get crowded in the summer, particularly at weekends. Those who prefer a solid roof over their heads can rent a bungalow.

Real Residência
MAP F1 ▪ Rua Ramalho Ortigão 41 ▪ 213 822 900 ▪ www.realhotelsgroup.com ▪ €
Comprising 22 suites and two studios, all with kitchenettes, this suite hotel stands just across the street from the Museu Calouste Gulbenkian

(see pp30–31), while Parque Eduardo VII is only a few blocks away. Guests can also access the health club at sister hotel the Real Palácio (see p114), which is located a bit further away.

Altis Prime
MAP F3 ▪ Rua Rodrigo da Fonseca 4 ▪ 210 456 000 ▪ www.altishotels.com ▪ €€
This centrally located, luxurious apartment hotel is spread over nine floors and offers on-site facilities including a rooftop sun deck, private parking and all the benefits of the five-star Altis Grand next door. All apartments and penthouses are well-equipped with a kitchenette, free Wi-Fi and a private bathroom.

Legendary Lisboa Suites
MAP F3 ▪ Rua Rodrigo da Fonseca 44 ▪ 210 046 600 ▪ www.legendarylisboasuites.com ▪ €€
This well-equipped mid-range hotel is to be found near the Marquês de Pombal roundabout. Standard suites are small and have kitchenettes. Grander penthouse suites are also available.

VIP Executive Éden Aparthotel
MAP L2 ▪ Praça dos Restauradores 24 ▪ 213 216 600 ▪ www.viphotels.com ▪ €€
Housed in what was once the grand Art Deco Eden theatre, overlooking Restauradores, this is Lisbon's most central and well-equipped apartment hotel. The decor is a little dated, but the rooftop pool offers great views over the city.

General Index

Acknowledgments

This edition updated by

Contributor Joana Taborda
Senior Editors Alison McGill, Lucy Richards
Project Editor Parnika Bagla
Senior Art Editor Vinita Venugopal
Editor Mark Silas
Assistant Editor Nandini Desiraju
Assistant Art Editor Divyanshi Shreyaskar
Picture Research Administrator Vagisha Pushp
Picture Research Manager Taiyaba Khatoon
Publishing Assistant Halima Mohammed
Jacket Designer Jordan Lambley
Senior Cartographer Subhashree Bharati
Cartography Manager Suresh Kumar
Senior DTP Designer Tanveer Zaidi
Senior Production Editor Jason Little
Senior Production Controller Kariss Ainsworth
Deputy Managing Editor Beverly Smart
Managing Editors Shikha Kulkarni, Hollie Teague
Managing Art Editor Sarah Snelling
Senior Managing Art Editor Priyanka Thakur
Art Director Maxine Pedliham
Publishing Director Georgina Dee

DK would like to thank the following for their contribution to the previous editions: Tomas Tranæus, Matthew Hancock, Hilary Bird, Linda Whitwam, Peter Wilson, Rough Guides/Natascha Sturny and Tony Souter.

The publisher would like to thank the following for their kind permission to reproduce their photographs:

(Key: a-above; b-below/bottom; c-centre; f-far; l-left; r-right; t-top)
100 Maneiras: Fabrice Demoulin 83crb.
123RF.com: joseelias 3tl, 10cla, 60-1; Arseniy Rogov 16-7.
4Corners: Maurício Abreu 96t; Michael Howard 4cla; SIME/Johanna Huber 2tr, 34-5, 88tl; SIME/Paolo Giocoso 12bl.
Alamy Stock Photo: AEP 26cl; age fotostock/José Antonio Moreno 58b, Juan Carlos Muñoz 78tl, /M&G Therin-Weise 62tr; Paulo Amorim 48t; Paulo Amorim/WWPics 105cr; Mieneke Andeweg-van Rijn 17crb; Art Directors & TRIP ArkReligion.com 68tl; Radu Bercan 48t; Pavel Dudek 88tl; Andrew Duke 10cl; Eric Farrelly 57br; Paul Gapper 46cb, 57tl; GM Photo Images 16cla; Hemis 91cr; Hemis/Anna Serrano 84tr; hemis.fr / Patrice Hauser 82b, / Ludovic Maisant 52tl, / Emilio Suetone 67crb; Peter Horree 86bl; Bjanka Kadic 51cl, 55br; John Kellerman 14crb, 14-5, 15tl; Cro Magnon 39br, 65clb, 80bl, 86tr; dov makabaw 81cla; Miguel Moya 70br; North Wind Picture Archives 36b; James O'Sullivan 4cl; Sean Pavone 59tr, 64b; REDA &CO srl/Michele Bella 75cr; Mauro Rodrigues 49cl; Sagaphoto.com/Forget Gautier 50b; Iain Sharp 85cra; Roman Sigaev 23tl; M. Sobreira 39cl; StockPhotosArt - Urban Landscape/Sofia Pereira 20-1, 79cl; SuperStock/Richard Cummins 16br; Mauro Toccaceli 53tr; Rachel Torres 64tr; Travel Pictures/Pictures Colour Library 77cla; UrbanTexture 50tc; Ivan Vdovin 6tr, 12cr, 14cla, 15br, 21tl; Kavalenkava Volha 1; Ken Welsh 4t, 11cra; Dudley Wood 26-7, 55tl.
Alecrim no Prato: 89crb.
Alma: 83cl.
Arte Rústica: 72cb.
AWL Images: Mauricio Abreu 45tr, 58tr; Michele Falzone 13cra.
Bar Lounge: 90tl.
Bridgeman Images: 37tr; Gerald Bloncourt 37cl.
Casa-Museu Fundação Medeiros e Almeida: 94cla, 95t.
Chapitô: 66t.
Centro Colombo: 98bl.
Confeiteria Nacional: 74cl.
Corbis: Mauricio Abreu 41tr, 47clb; JAI/Alan Copson 13tl; JAI/Mauricio Abreu 6cr; Frank Krahmer 45cl; Holger Leue 49tr; Sylvain Sonnet 27crb, 77br.
Direcão-Geral do Património Cultural/Arquivo de Documentação Fotográfica(DGPC/ADF): Francisco Arruda/Luis Pava âoBaluarte 23clb; Museu Nacional dos Coches 38b; Museu Nacional de Antiga 18-9; Museu Nacional de Arte Antiga, Lisboa Instituto dos Museus e da Conservação - MC 10cb, 19crb, 38tl; Museu Nacional do Azulejo/Luísa Oliveira 2014 27tl.
Dreamstime.com: Allexander 34-5c; Luis Alvarenga 87cl; Leonid Andronov 46bl; Bastabla 63tr; Artur Bogacki 56bl; Olena Buyskykh 101b; Carlos Caetano 44tr; Henner Damke 41clb; Phil Darby 54br; Ionut David 40bl; Dirk123 84cla; Emicristea 69b, 70cl; Rob Van Esch 17tl, 24-5; Europhotos 92-3; Farbregas 42t; Greta Gabaglio 78cra; Dan Grytsku 48bl; Gvictoria 11tl, 22-3; Ideastud 4clb; Joyfull 101tr; Vichaya Kiatying-angsulee 71cla; Martin Lehmann 4crb; Artem Merzlenko 4b, 6cla; Juan Moyano 3tr, 106-7; Sean Pavone 100tl; Radub85 21br; Antonio Ribeiro 22clb; Arseniy Rogov 102cl; Saiko3p 32-3; Sam74100 43tr, 44b, 46t, 56tl; Rui G. Santos 96b; Jose I. Soto 2tl, 8-9; Stevanzz 95br, 104clb; Rui Vale De Sousa 4cra; Val_th 33crb; Stefano Valeri 69tl; Vlat456 103tl; Zts 10bl, 40tr, 54cla, 59cl, 97cla, Zts 74br.

Fundação Calouste Gulbenkian, Lisbon:
11cb, 30clb, 30-1, 31tl, 31ca, 31crb.
Fundação Millennium bcp : Núcleo
Arqueológico 56cr.
Hospital de Bonecas: Nick Sinclai 73crb.
Getty Images: DEA / G. DAGLI ORTI 36tr.
Leitão & Irmão: 80ca.
Museu da Marioneta: Diogo Ferreira 86cla.
Museu Rafael Bordalo Pinheiro: 98cra.
Parreirinha de Alfama: 51tr.
**Parques de Sintra - Monte da Lua,
S.A.(PSML):** 32clb; Emigus 11b, 32cla, 33tl,
102br; Palácio de Queluz/ Carlos Pombo
11clb; Wilson Pereira 28-9, 29br, 104tl.
Rex by Shutterstock: Lydia Evans 18clb;
imageBROKER/Silvana Guilhermino 13bc;
Robert Harding/Michael Runkel 43bl.
Robert Harding Picture Library: Andre
Goncalves 78b.
Station Restaurant & Club: Matos Fernandes
50tl.
Teatro Nacional Dona Maria II: Ana Paula
Carvalho 72tl.
Thema Hotels & Resorts: Eleven 53cla, 99cr.

Cover:
Front and spine: **Alamy Stock Photo:**
Kavalenkava Volha.

Back: **Alamy Stock Photo:** Ian Dagnall crb,
Kavalenkava Volha b; **Dreamstime.com:**
Joyfull tr, Jose I. Soto tl; **Getty Images:**
Moment / Alexander Spatari cla.

Pull Out Map Cover:
Alamy Stock Photo: Kavalenkava Volha.

All other images © Dorling Kindersley
For further information see:
www.dkimages.com

Illustrator Chapel Design & Marketing
First edition created by Coppermill Books,
London.

Penguin
Random
House

First edition 2007
First published in Great Britain by
Dorling Kindersley Limited,
DK, One Embassy Gardens, 8 Viaduct
Gardens, London SW11 7BW, UK
The authorised representative in the EEA is
Dorling Kindersley Verlag GmbH. Arnulfstr.
124, 80636 Munich, Germany

Published in the United States by
DK Publishing, 1745 Broadway, 20th Floor,
New York, NY 10019, USA
Copyright © 2007, 2023
Dorling Kindersley Limited
A Penguin Random House Company
23, 24, 25, 26 10 9 8 7 6 5 4 3 2 1

A CIP catalogue record is available
from the British Library.
A catalogue record for this book is available
from the Library of Congress.
ISSN 1479-344X
ISBN 978-0-2416-1873-8
Printed and bound in Malaysia

www.dk.com

*As a guide to abbreviations in visitor information
blocks:* **Adm** *= admission charge;* **D** *= dinner,*
L *= lunch.*

MIX
Paper | Supporting
responsible forestry
FSC™ C018179

This book was made with Forest
Stewardship Council™ certified
paper – one small step in DK's
commitment to a sustainable future.
**For more information go to
www.dk.com/our-green-pledge**

Phrase Book

In an Emergency

Help!	**Socorro!**	soo-koh-roo
Stop!	**Pare!**	pahr'
Call a doctor!	**Chame um médico!**	shahm' ooñ meh-dee-koo
Call an ambulance!	**Chame uma ambulância!**	shahm' oo-muh añ-boo-lañ-see-uh
Call the police!	**Chame a polícia!**	shahm' uh poo-lee-see-uh
Call the fire brigade!	**Chame os bombeiros!**	shahm' oosh bom-bay-roosh

Communication Essentials

Yes	**Sim**	seeñ
No	**Não**	nowñ
Please	**Por favor/ Faz favor**	poor fuh-vor/ fash fuh-vor
Thank you	**Obrigado/da**	o-bree-gah-doo/duh
Excuse me	**Desculpe**	dish-koolp'
Hello	**Olá**	oh-lah
Goodbye	**Adeus**	a-deh-oosh
Yesterday	**Ontem**	oñ-tayñ
Today	**Hoje**	ohj'
Tomorrow	**Amanhã**	ah-mañ-yañ
Here	**Aqui**	uh-kee
There	**Ali**	uh-lee
What?	**O quê?**	oo keh
Which	**Qual?**	kwahl'
When?	**Quando?**	kwañ-doo
Why?	**Porquê?**	poor-keh
Where?	**Onde?**	oñd'

Useful Phrases

How are you?	**Como está?**	koh-moo shtah
Very well, thank you	**Bem, obrigado/da.**	bayñ o-bree-gah-doo/duh
Where is/are ...?	**Onde está/estão ...?**	ond' shtah/ shtowñ
How far is it to ...?	**A que distância fica . . . ?**	uh kee dish-tañ-see-uh fee-kuh
Which way to ...?	**Como se vai para . . . ?**	koh-moo seh vy puh-ruh
Do you speak English?	**Fala inglês?**	fah-luh eeñ-glehsh
I don't understand	**Não compreendo**	nowñ kom-pree-eñ-doo
Could you speak more slowly please?	**Pode falar mais devagar por favor?**	pohd' fuh-lar mysh d'-va-gar poor fuh-vor
I'm sorry	**Desculpe**	dish-koolp'

Useful Words

big	**grande**	grañd'
small	**pequeno**	pe-keh-noo
hot	**quente**	keñt'
cold	**frio**	free-oo
good	**bom**	boñ
bad	**mau**	mah-oo
open	**aberto**	a-behr-too
closed	**fechado**	fe-shah-doo
left	**esquerda**	shkeh-duh
right	**direita**	dee-ray-tuh
straight on	**em frente**	ayñ freñt'
near	**perto**	pehr-too
far	**longe**	loñj'
up	**para cima**	pur-ruh see-muh
down	**para baixo**	pur-ruh buy-shoo
early	**cedo**	seh-doo

late	**tarde**	tard'
entrance	**entrada**	eñ-trah-duh
exit	**saída**	sa-ee-duh
toilets	**casa de banho**	kah-zuh d' bañ-yoo
more	**mais**	mysh
less	**menos**	meh-noosh

Shopping

How much does this cost?	**Quanto custa isto?**	kwañ-too koosh-tuh eesh-too
I would like ...	**Queria ...**	kree-uh
I'm just looking	**Estou só a ver obrigado/a**	shtoh soh uh vehr o-bree-gah-doo/uh
Do you take credit cards?	**Aceita cartões de crédito?**	uh-say-tuh kar-toinsh de kreh-dee-too
What time do you open?	**A que horas abre?**	uh kee oh-rash ah-bre
What time do you close?	**A que horas fecha?**	uh kee oh-rash fay-shuh
This/that one	**Este/Esse**	ehst'/ehss'
expensive	**caro**	kah-roo
cheap	**barato**	buh-rah-too
size	**tamanho**	ta-man-yoo
white	**branco**	brañ-koo
black	**preto**	preh-too
red	**vermelho**	ver-mehl-yoo
yellow	**amarelo**	uh-muh-reh-loo
green	**verde**	vehrd'
blue	**azul**	uh-zool'
bakery	**padaria**	pah-duh-ree-uh
bank	**banco**	bañ-koo
bookshop	**livraria**	lee-vruh-ree-uh
cake shop	**pastelaria**	pash-te-luh-ree-uh
chemist	**farmácia**	far-mah-see-uh
market	**mercado**	mehr-kah-doo
newsagent	**quiosque**	kee-yohsk'
post office	**correios**	koo-ray-oosh

Sightseeing

cathedral	**sé**	seh
church	**igreja**	ee-gray-juh
garden	**jardim**	jar-deeñ
library	**biblioteca**	bee-blee-oo-teh-kuh
museum	**museu**	moo-zeh-oo
tourist information office	**posto de turismo**	posh-too d' too-reesh-moo
bus station	**estação de autocarros**	shta-sowñ d' oh-too-kah-roosh
railway station	**estação de comboios**	shta-sowñ d' koñ-boy-oosh

Staying in a Hotel

Do you have a vacant room?	**Tem um quarto livre?**	tayñ ooñ kwar-too leevr'
room with a bath	**um quarto com casa de banho**	ooñ kwar-too koñ kah-zuh d' bañ-yoo
shower	**duche**	doosh
single room	**quarto individual**	kwar-too een-dee-vee-doo-ahl'
double room	**quarto de casal**	kwar-too d' kuh-zahl'
twin room	**quarto com duas camas**	kwar-too koñ doo-ash kah-mash
I have a reservation	**Tenho um quarto reservado**	tayñ-yoo ooñ kwar-too re-ser-vah-doo

Eating Out

Have you got a table for ...?	**Tem uma mesa para ... ?**	*tayñ oo-muh meh-zuh puh-ruh*
I want to reserve a table	**Quero reservar uma mesa**	*keh-roo re-zehr-var o-muh meh-zuh*
The bill, please	**A conta por favor/ faz favor**	*uh kohn-tuh poor fuh-vor/ fash fuh-vor*
I am a vegetarian	**Sou vegetariano/a**	*Soh ve-je-tuh-ree-ah-noo/uh*
the menu	**a lista**	*uh leesh-tuh*
wine list	**a lista de vinhos**	*uh leesh-tuh de veeñ-yoosh*
glass	**um copo**	*ooñ koh-poo*
bottle	**uma garrafa**	*oo-muh guh-rah-fuh*
knife	**uma faca**	*oo-muh fah-kuh*
fork	**um garfo**	*ooñ gar-foo*
spoon	**uma colher**	*oo-muh kool-yair*
plate	**um prato**	*ooñ prah-too*
breakfast	**pequeno- almoço**	*pe-keh-noo- ahl-moh-soo*
lunch	**almoço**	*ahl-moh-soo*
dinner	**jantar**	*jan-tar*
starter	**entrada**	*eñ-trah-duh*
main course	**prato principal**	*prah-too prin-see-pahl'*
dessert	**sobremesa**	*soh-bre-meh-zuh*
rare	**mal passado**	*mahl' puh-sah-doo*
medium	**médio**	*meh-dee-oo*
well done	**bem passado**	*bayñ puh-sah-doo*

Menu Decoder

açorda	*uh-sor-duh*	bread-based stew
açúcar	*uh-soo-kar*	sugar
água mineral	*ah-gwuh mee-ne-rahl'*	mineral water
com gás	*koñ gas*	sparkling
sem gás	*sayñ gas*	still
alho	*al-yoo*	garlic
amêijoas	*uh-may-joo-ash*	clams
arroz	*uh-rohsh*	rice
atum	*uh-tooñ*	tuna
azeitonas	*uh-zay-toh-nash*	olives
bacalhau	*buh-kuh-lyow*	dried, salted cod
batatas	*buh-tah-tash*	potatoes
batatas fritas	*buh-tah-tash free-tash*	French fries
bica	*bee-kuh*	espresso
bife	*beef*	steak
bolo	*boh-loo*	cake
borrego	*boo-reh-goo*	lamb
café	*kuh-feh*	coffee
camarões	*kuh-muh-roysh*	shrimp
caranguejo	*kuh-rañ-gay-joo*	crab
carne	*karn'*	meat
cebola	*se-boh-luh*	onion
cerveja	*sehr-vay-juh*	beer
chouriço	*shoh-ree-soo*	red, spicy sausage
cogumelos	*koo-goo-meh-loosh*	mushrooms
~~f~~ambre	*fee-añbr'*	ham
~~f~~gado	*fee-guh-doo*	liver
~~fra~~ngo	*frañ-goo*	chicken
	free-too	fried
	froo-tuh	fruit
	gam-bash	prawns
	je-lah-doo	ice cream
	jeh-loo	ice
	grel-yah-d	grilled
	muh-sañ	apple
	mañ-tay-guh	butter
	muh-reesh-koosh	seafood
	osh-trash	oysters

ovos	*oh-voosh*	eggs
pão	*powñ*	bread
pastel	*pash-tehl'*	pastry
pato	*pah-too*	duck
peixe	*paysh'*	fish
pimenta	*pee-meñ-tuh*	pepper
polvo	*pohl'-voo*	octopus
porco	*por-coo*	pork
queijo	*kay-joo*	cheese
sal	*sahl'*	salt
salada	*suh-lah-duh*	salad
salsichas	*sahl-see-shash*	sausages
sopa	*soh-puh*	soup
sumo	*soo-moo*	juice
tamboril	*tañ-boo-ril'*	monkfish
tomate	*too-maht'*	tomato
vinho branco	*veeñ-yoo brañ-koo*	white wine
vinho tinto	*veeñ-yoo teeñ-too*	red wine
vitela	*vee-teh-luh*	veal

Numbers

0	**zero**	*zeh-roo*
1	**um**	*ooñ*
2	**dois**	*doysh*
3	**três**	*tresh*
4	**quatro**	*kwa-troo*
5	**cinco**	*seeñ-koo*
6	**seis**	*saysh*
7	**sete**	*set'*
8	**oito**	*oy-too*
9	**nove**	*nov'*
10	**dez**	*desh*
11	**onze**	*oñz'*
12	**doze**	*doz'*
13	**treze**	*trez'*
14	**catorze**	*ka-torz'*
15	**quinze**	*keeñz'*
16	**dezasseis**	*de-zuh-saysh*
17	**dezassete**	*de-zuh-set'*
18	**dezoito**	*de-zoy-too*
19	**dezanove**	*de-zuh-nov'*
20	**vinte**	*veent'*
21	**vinte e um**	*veen-tee-ooñ*
30	**trinta**	*treeñ-tuh*
40	**quarenta**	*kwa-reñ-tuh*
50	**cinquenta**	*seen-kweñ-tuh*
60	**sessenta**	*se-señ-tuh*
70	**setenta**	*se-teñ-tuh*
80	**oitenta**	*oy-teñ-tuh*
90	**noventa**	*noo-veñ-tuh*
100	**cem**	*sayñ*
101	**cento e um**	*señ-too-ee-ooñ*
200	**duzentos**	*doo-zeñ-toosh*
300	**trezentos**	*tre-zeñ-toosh*
400	**quatrocentos**	*kwa-troo- señ-toosh*
500	**quinhentos**	*kee-nyeñ-toosh*
700	**setecentos**	*set'-señ-toosh*
900	**novecentos**	*nov'-señ-toosh*
1,000	**mil**	*meel'*

Time

one minute	**um minuto**	*ooñ mee-noo-too*
one hour	**uma hora**	*oo-muh oh-ruh*
half an hour	**meia-hora**	*may-uh-oh-ruh*
Monday	**segunda-feira**	*se-goon- duh-fay-ruh*
Tuesday	**terça-feira**	*ter-sa-fay-ruh*
Wednesday	**quarta-feira**	*kwar-ta-fay-ruh*
Thursday	**quinta-feira**	*keen-ta-fay-ruh*
Friday	**sexta-feira**	*say-shta-fay-ruh*
Saturday	**sábado**	*sah-ba-doo*
Sunday	**domingo**	*doo-meen-goo*

Lisbon Street Index